THE PADEL PLAYER'S GUIDE

ELEVATE YOUR GAME NO MATTER YOUR LEVEL

SANDY FARQUHARSON

WWW.THEPADELSCHOOL.COM

Copyright © 2024 by Sandy Farquharson

All rights reserved.

No part of this publication may be reproduced in any form, or by any means, electronic or mechanical, including photocopying, recording, or any information browsing, storage, or retrieval system, without permission in writing from the author.

Cover and Book Design: Mariella Travis | www.alleiram.com

ISBN
978-1-3999-7924-5

DISCLAIMER

Although the author and publisher have made every effort to ensure that the information in this book was correct at press time, the author does not assume and hereby disclaims any liability to any party for any loss, damage, or disruption caused by errors, or omissions, whether such errors or omissions result from negligence, accident, or any other cause.

Author further disclaims any liability for any party for the self-help advice and opinions on said subjects contained within this book. The information provided in this book is designed to provide helpful information on the subjects discussed.

Copyright © 2024 The Padel School

All Rights Reserved

Table of Contents

Disclaimer iii

Introduction *A Padel Journey* 1

Quick! Split Step! Stop Here Before You Continue. 9

Stage One *Momentous Discovery & Escalating Enjoyment* 11

   Chapter One *Our Padel Journey Begins* 13

   Chapter Two *Master Your Understanding of the Game* 23

   Chapter Three *Skills for a Solid Foundation* 46

   Chapter Four *Ramping Up Your Intensity and Frequency of Play* 54

   Chapter Five *Clothing, Basic Equipment, Rackets, and Shoes* 61

   Chapter Six *Basic Improvements You Must Make Before You Advance* 66

Stage Two *Rapid Improvement & Breakthrough* 77

   Chapter Seven *Play to Improve* 79

   Chapter Eight *Reading and Controlling Your Match* 89

   Chapter Nine *Don't Let the Plateau Stop You* 101

   Chapter Ten *Begin Your Domination* 115

Stage Three *High-Level Competition* 133

   Chapter Eleven *Elevate* 135

   Chapter Twelve *High-Level Competition Skills and Tactics* 147

   Conclusion *The Next Step of Your Journey* 161

   Everything You Need to Take the Next Step in Your Padel Journey. 164

   A Quick Favour? 165

   About the Author 166

Introduction
A Padel Journey

"Right now my obsession beats talent, really. My dream is to train every day and learn something, [to] take something new with me that allows me to improve my passion."

—Juan Lebrón

There are moments on every padel journey where it all seems to come together. In this split second, a circuit in your mind completes and you finally succeed. The tactic you've been trying to implement actually works in a match… You finally understand how to defend the double glass rebound… You successfully hit a winning vibora into the corner… You run out of the court to defend a smash… Your moment started as a small seed of potential, and then blossomed into something incredible.

A typical padel journey is mired in many of these small moments. The problem? They're not always fun. Sometimes, it takes a loss in a tournament or a swollen arm in order to recognize the need for a break. Other times, it takes a golden point match point in order to truly test your mettle. Sometimes, you experience your padel epiphany through major frustration.

My phone lit up with a text from my friend Sam. *"Hey Sandy! Ultimate frisbee Saturday at four. You in?"*

"Sure, I'll be there," I shot back as a broad grin crossed my face.

I loved ultimate frisbee and couldn't wait to play. I had no idea this one game would change everything, for good and for ill.

I joined my friends on the field and revelled in the intensity of the frisbee match. Nothing gets your heart pumping quite like running, diving, and otherwise going all out to score a point for your team. I was unstoppable on the field, until I wasn't. I jumped high to reach for the floating disc among too many players and came down awkwardly on my knee. You probably know how this story ends: I tore my ACL. Besides the abrupt end to my casual relationship with ultimate frisbee, my career in padel would face an uphill battle for the next several years, all because of one small accident.

When you hurt yourself like I did, the first thoughts to pop into your head are all the events you'll no longer be able to attend, the sports you won't be able to play, and the time you'll lose. The pain is secondary to what this accident costs you in lost time and missed opportunities. I knew my goal to compete for my third straight title in the NAS Ramadan padel tournament in Dubai was now impossible. There's no speedy recovery for an ACL, and since the tournament was just around the corner, I knew I would be sitting on the sidelines as a spectator.

I set out on my nine-month recovery in good spirits. I was extremely disappointed, but what was there to do besides grin and bear it? I pushed hard, working every day with an intensity that would frighten passersby if they looked too closely through the glass windows of my gym. My goal was to time my recovery to reclaim my title in the Ramadan tournament the following year. I would compete, and I would win. These thoughts propelled me forward and kept me sane on all those days inside while I sat on the couch with my knee wrapped in ice. It was this driving force and will to compete that kept me going and ultimately sped my recovery, even when things took a turn for the worse...

At month seven of rehab, a feeling of increasing dread grew deep within me. I knew something was wrong. I wanted to ignore it and hope for the best, but when the recovery still wasn't progressing as my doctor and I expected, they did another scan of my knee. Turns out the doctors hadn't performed the surgery properly. I then had to get not one, but two separate surgeries to correct the error. So yeah, please don't ever kick me in the knee even as a joke. I'm not sure it would take the pressure.

At about the year mark I was nowhere near completely healed, but that wouldn't stop me. I stepped onto the court at the Ramadan tournament having not even hit a ball in over a year. I was representing His Highness Sheikh Saeed and it meant a lot for me to even be able to step on the court. I was undertrained and not at my best physically, but I was ready to give it everything I had. Still, my partner, Javier Lopez, would need to play at 110% for us to even have a chance. Luckily for us, he played incredibly well throughout the event.

I learned early in the tournament what my knee could and couldn't do. I could run up to the net, move back to the glass as needed, but let's just say the other teams weren't quaking in their boots. In fact, judging by their relentless targeting of me, they seemed excited to have a real chance. I didn't blame them, I would have done the same thing in their shoes. Still, they sorely tested my stamina and ability to stand upright on both legs.

After fighting through tears of pain, sweat, and a few starry-eyed moments, my partner and I impossibly made it to the finals. By this time, my knee looked like Cristiano Ronaldo kicked a football directly into it, lodging just below my kneecap. I was in quite a bit of pain, but I was ready to do whatever it took to win, even if that meant having to strategize around my immobility.

I'm at my best when I am reactive, fast to net, and attacking. With a knee the size of a watermelon, this type of game just wasn't possible. During our pre-game strategy chat, Javier and I decided I would play a more defensive game from the back and my partner would take the lead on the attack. I would only come in at select times to maximise efficiency while minimising my movements. So, in pain but with a plan, he jumped onto the court and I hobbled in behind him.

Each point was a major struggle. The pain in my leg only intensified as the match went on. The last thing you want when you're injured is to suffer prolonged rallies and have to fight for every point, but there was no other option. Sensing my weakness and immobility, our opponents played most of the points on me, forcing me to stay in the back and defend like my life depended on it. My partner stepped up and played some of the best padel I'd ever seen from him, while I did everything I could to keep us in the game.

And then, like a lightning bolt, it hit me...

An epiphany took root in my mind...

Everything I'd thought and believed up until this point about the game was reversed...

I knew, without a shadow of a doubt, that padel was largely mental and tactical. I had no right to be in the finals in my condition, and yet I was there and we weren't horribly losing. This electric surge of inspiration spurred me to be consistent, make no mistakes, slow the game down, hit plenty of lobs, and just buy myself as much time as possible to reset between each rally.

Competing on the padel circuit in Dubai.

It came down to the wire, but we just barely managed to squeak by and take the last set 7-5. As soon as the point was over, I collapsed onto the court, hugging my partner. It was a win in so many wonderful ways. I joined the tournament hoping to represent, but I wasn't confident I would be able to muster the fortitude needed to overcome my injury. I was as surprised as anyone that we even made it to the finals. However, thousands of tennis matches in high-pressure situations taught me to never give up and to fight until the very end. Looking back now, I wish I could have skipped the pain and frustration of tearing my ACL, but it forced me to learn an invaluable padel lesson. I always knew how important the technical aspects of the game were for improvement, but this experience made me realise that winning matches is also about the mental and tactical. All sides of the game need to come together for a player to unlock their potential.

The Three Stages of the Padel Journey

After training hundreds of students in a variety of countries, I've come across a vast spectrum of padel players. With the exception of outliers, 99% of players will travel through each of the following three stages. Each player's journey is unique, and time spent in each will vary, but once you understand exactly where you currently fit, you'll be able to take your game to the next level. We'll cover each stage in-depth in this book.

1. **Stage One: Momentous Discovery & Escalating Enjoyment:** This is the wonderful stage when padel is a new sport some friends asked you to try. You're discovering it for the first time and find immense enjoyment from day one. You are already in love with padel and are starting to play one to two times per week, but your skills and tactics are still in the beginner stage.

2. **Stage Two: Rapid Improvement & Breakthrough:** You've started in-person coaching and watching online resources and you're rapidly improving and inching towards intermediate level play. You play padel regularly without injury. Your level continuously advances and you are thinking about joining either a league or challenging yourself in a tournament.

3. **Stage Three: High-Level Competition:** You're starting to play in social and/or professional competitions and have specific goals. You've shattered plateaus and your level continuously improves.

What stage are you in? Honest reflection will do wonders for your potential advancement. Each stage represents an important progression point on the padel journey. Some players skip ahead too fast and end up competing before they've mastered important parts of each stage. You may even have some people who come to mind who are already competing, but lack an understanding of the importance of basic strategies like taking the net. Some players skip ahead to making padel a way of life too soon and find themselves facing burnout, sudden disinterest, or injury. It's important to take an honest look at your own journey to craft your personal plan for improvement. This book will help you do that.

Your personal journey won't be a linear path. You might even try to jump to high-level competition without the firm foundation gained from going through stages one and two. In each chapter of this book, you'll learn the ideal progression for a player on the padel journey, but yours might be wildly different. Don't sweat it, you can always go back to the drawing board if you need to. Determine your way forward by navigating around common errors and making consistent progress.

When all is said and done, enjoy each stage you're in while you're there. There's no need to rush your improvement so much that you don't have fun at each stage. Savour the padel journey and bask in the pure joy of getting on court.

Get the Most Out of This Book

You picked up this book because you want to improve. You want to be able to beat your friends, win some local tournaments, and maybe even look good doing it. You also want to avoid injury for the very real reason that injuries mean you can't play padel as often. You want to know how to improve specific areas of your padel game and find out what you're missing. You're not afraid of doing what needs to be done to break bad habits and form lasting skills.

I wrote this book to appeal to many different types of players. If you're a beginner to padel, welcome. This book is a fantastic place to start as it contains everything you need to know. If you're a padel veteran you might be tempted to skip right to the competition stage at the end. While I won't stop you, I do offer a word of caution: When players fail to advance and get stuck at a frustrating plateau, it's often because they missed out on the basics. If you're one of these players, you may have come up with a workaround that has worked so far, but you'll eventually get stuck because of flawed technique or bad tactics. One simple change might be all you need to elevate your game.

You'll read about the many mistakes I've made on my journey, as well as errors I've seen other players make. It's my goal to help you avoid these same painful mistakes. The best players are willing to grow through failure, but typically don't get stuck for very long. If there is a part of your game sorely lacking, this book is the place to start.

As you track the common journey in this book, consider your personal goals. Be intentional with your padel journey and what you need to do to advance your stage. Think about how far you want to go and we'll get there together.

If you're ready, let's run onto the court and hit a few balls.

Get on the Court

*At the end of each chapter, I'll prompt you to reflect on one aspect of your padel game, and then take action to improve. It's important to take this time to step back, reflect on your personal journey, and then make progress accordingly. You could devour this book in one sitting, but it might be hard to remember all the skills and tactics you will learn. Take a moment, grab a pen or device, and take a moment to answer questions as you read. Pick one specific skill or technique to practise, go to a court, and then come back after you've made progress.

Reflection: *Consider the strongest and weakest areas of your padel game and ask yourself two questions:*

1. *What's one skill I really need to improve if I am going to advance further?*

2. *What is the strongest part of my game?*

Action: *Considering your answers to the above, come prepared for your next lesson or match with friends and focus on improving one aspect of your game.*

Quick! Split Step! Stop Here Before You Continue...

Head on over to ThePadelSchool.com to join our growing padel community. Elevate your game right away by sharing shotfixer videos, getting feedback from our coaches, and interacting with like-minded padel enthusiasts. This is where the team spends most of its time online!

We can't wait to see you there,

—Sandy and The Padel School Team

Stage One

Momentous Discovery & Escalating Enjoyment

Chapter One
Our Padel Journey Begins

In life, just find something you love and make it your life. That is the only way to be successful. Love what you do.

—'Hurricane Hannah' Cockcroft

I'm Sandy Farquharson, the founder of The Padel School, an online platform that helps players and coaches unlock their padel potential. Just like you, I love this game. My padel journey began in 2012, long before I hurt my knee playing frisbee. I lived in the incredible city of Dubai teaching tennis with an academy. Even though I loved this beautiful place, it was time for me to move on and continue my tennis journey elsewhere. I decided tennis in that setting was no longer quite the right fit for me so I quit my job, sold all my furniture, cancelled my visas, and completed the demanding process of leaving the country to return home. I was all set and ready to leave, but padel got in the way.

"Hey mate, want to play a game of tennis later today?" I asked my friend Simon, who happened to be an excellent squash player.

Simon responded with a dry grin and an almost imperceptible roll of his eyes. "Not really. Last time we played you destroyed me. It wasn't even fun…"

"Come on, I'll take it easy on you!" I responded, not wanting to lose out on the chance for a fun game.

This time Simon really did roll his eyes and said, "How about we play squash instead?"

Now it was my turn to groan. "Why would I do that? Last time we played I was sore for a week. I can't keep up with you."

He smiled and said, "Well, why don't we give padel a try? It looks like it could be fun."

Simon and I often had discussions like this. I played at a much higher level than he did in tennis, and he was incredibly strong in squash. We enjoyed competing against each other in both sports, but our levels just weren't compatible for either sport to be competitive. We weren't sure what to do.

Padel was relatively new in Dubai. We knew about it, but hadn't yet played. There were two public courts nearby and we thought, okay, let's give it a go. What did we have to lose? It looked like something both of us could play and we could find a middle ground with our skills at racket sports. So we played a friendly match and didn't really think anything of it at the time. It was good fun and Simon and I were able to compete, but I was still going back to the UK to pursue tennis. Padel didn't have a hold over me. Yet…

A week before I left, a major team competition took place in Dubai. Every year during Ramadan, Sheikh Hamdan, the Crown Prince of Dubai (and padel aficionado), holds a tournament. One of the players dropped out and they invited me to come and play.

With His Highness Sheikh Hamdan bin Mohammed bin Rashid Al Maktoum

My first thought was, *Joke's on them! I've only played padel once!* But with my tennis background and general knack for rapid learning, I was confident enough to say yes. The only problem? My flight out of the country was the same time as the finals! But we wouldn't really need to worry about that, right? Wrong...

As you might have guessed, our team played extremely well and we made the final. But I was in a pickle. Do I fly back and leave everything behind or stay to help my team win? I knew what I wanted to do, my competitive personality is quite strong, but it wouldn't be easy to change plans last minute. I was enjoying myself more than I expected and I really wanted to see the competition through to the end, but it still felt wrong to miss or change flights. Luckily, the team sponsor stepped in and made my decision easy.

They paid for my flight change and figured out all the details for me so I could focus on the competition. I'm forever grateful for their help and support. I went to the final match with bags packed as my plane home was set to lift off mere hours afterwards. It was a close match, but my team pulled out the victory in the end. Being part of something so momentous was an amazing and almost indescribable experience.

Winners of the Ramadan Padel Tournament presented by His Highness Sheikh Saeed bin Maktoum bin Juma Al Maktoum (aka Uncle Saeed).

Right after the game, I spoke to the management of the club and they said, "Sandy, look, we loved what you did for your team. It was excellent to watch! We need a rackets manager. Would you be interested?"

I sent them my CV straightaway, which was conveniently set up for exactly the role they needed and told them, "Look, I'm not really looking for something at the moment. I've got something in the UK I'm pretty much set on, and I have a plane to catch here…"

As I picked up my bags and headed off to the airport, I didn't think much more of it. I was still reeling from the emotional high of winning and trying to muster the energy required to travel. However, while rushing to catch my plane, I got a call from one of the directors at the club and he said, "Sandy, I know you're on your way to a flight, but we didn't want to let you get away. If you want the job, it's yours. You're exactly what this club needs. Will you be the new rackets manager for NAS Sports Complex?"

I recovered quickly from my surprise and said, "I have to really think about it because, for me, there's no tennis at the club and I'm not quite sure I'm qualified to coach padel. As you know, I've only played a few times! I don't really know it well enough to train others. If you were to send me for training, then I would strongly consider taking the job, but I don't want to say yes without training."

The discussion ended there for a time and I came back to miserable weather in the UK. The tennis scene also felt negative and it wasn't what I was hoping for. The battle in my mind was to continue down my path of working with elite tennis players in quite a political environment (but also what I was used to and where my knowledge was strong) or take a chance on a sport nobody had heard of, but that I felt was fun and sociable. I saw great potential in padel, but there was nowhere to learn about it in English.

The decision wasn't easy, but a few weeks later I was back in Dubai. They won me over by letting me take my training into my own hands and arranging my education the way I wanted. After orientation, they stayed true to their word and, upon my request, they sent me to Madrid for padel coach education. I went for two weeks, and I completed my first coach education course with the godfather of padel himself, Horacio Clementi, the coach almost all professional players look up to and admire. He played professionally and was ranked number one in the world for four years running. Suffice it to say, he knows his way around a padel court.

I really had no idea what I was walking into, but it felt like the perfect next step. I wasn't looking for it, but padel wormed its way right into my life.

Defining Your Unique Padel Journey

This was my entry into padel. Your story might be similar or completely different. You might have been born with a racket in your hand like me, or maybe you never played a sport before you found padel. No matter how you got your start, you're already a part of this amazing community of players. Welcome. We're glad to have you.

So what do you want your journey to look like?

Whatever you decide, you've made a great choice. I've trained business professionals who just wanted to crush their counterparts in a match. I've worked with parents who want to share their love of the game with their kids. I've trained people who just want to have a strong smash to impress their friends. I've also taught highly dedicated individuals who will stop at nothing to enter the competitive padel circuit to compete for their countries. No choice is any greater than the rest, but it's important you know your answer.

> *A good friend of mine recommended I play. I was not convinced but the first time I played, I was very frustrated but hooked. Since my best days of tennis had passed, padel had some of the same grittiness as a real tennis match. And the social side of it was great, too.* —Kent Seton, Los Angeles, member of The Padel School Community

Every player coming to the sport settles on their reason for playing. Whether you know it or not, you have a particular reason for showing up three to five times a week to play your favourite game. The good news? You'll know your reason and motivation for padel after reading this book. Figuring out your "why" for padel isn't just nice to know, it's crucial for deciding what type of player you want to be. It's not up to me or your coach to tell you where you want to go with padel. It's up to you.

As a coach, I know player motivations are vital. It's important I know where the player *wants* to go before I show them *how* to get there. If you don't know where you're going, you can't get there. Ask yourself three vital questions to visualise your own padel journey, and write your answers in your journal, or right here on this page:

1. Why do I like padel?

2. Why am I playing?

3. Why do I want to improve?

Your answers might blend together, and that's okay. But without a clear reason for playing padel, you'll eventually burn out, feel the bitter twang of injury, and/or stop playing altogether. But your answer needn't be, "so I can compete in the World Padel Tour," or, "so I can coach others one day." Playing padel because you love smashing the ball around after a stressful day at work is a perfectly acceptable answer.

There are many reasons to play padel, and your reason might be a mix of the following:

- **Social goals:** Padel is almost always played in pairs. The nature of the game contributes to the formation of close-knit groups where people play and compete. Many players find their home with like-minded padel enthusiasts.

- **Fitness goals:** Padel, like tennis and squash, will help you meet fitness goals. When your level rises, your rallies often last for several minutes during which you and your partner hardly stop moving. And then, after the point finally finishes, the next begins within seconds. You have just enough time for a deep breath before the game begins anew.

- **Stress relief:** Some players just want to smash the ball as hard as they can, as often as possible. They get immense pleasure and satisfaction from the physical release of hitting something. As you compete at a higher level, play in back-and-forth matches, and fight for every point, you're tuned into the moment. Endorphins rise and you feel like you can conquer the world.

- **Strategy:** Many players love the deep tactical side of padel that develops the longer you play. However, strategy begins as early as your first game. You have to figure out where to stand, how to read your opponents, and decide where to hit your next shot. Strategists are in the zone in this highly intellectual game.

- **Love of competition:** In the first stage of padel, you may encounter fierce competition if that is what you're looking for. Even if no one knows how to hit a bandeja, unforced errors reign supreme; or if you avoid letting the ball bounce off the glass, the match can still be competitive. Padel can be competitive at every stage as long as you play with people who match your level and competitive nature.

There's a certain ecstasy that comes from finally finding a sport that fits perfectly for you. For many, discovering padel was a momentous occasion that changed the way they felt about sports. Suddenly, there is a sport that leaves you feeling both refreshed and exhausted. For most, padel is much more often a hardcore passion than a casual hobby. Most people who play aren't content to play one match every few weeks, they want more.

Love at First Smash: The Allure of Padel

Padel is more than just a sport. It's a way of life.

When you're not playing, you're thinking about the next game. The anticipation of a match is like waiting for Father Christmas to pop down the chimney on Christmas Eve. But you don't have to wait until Christmas; just text a few friends, book a court, and you're all set for several hours of fun. As you wait for gametime, it's not uncommon to text your friends back and forth talking trash and otherwise building anticipation.

Padel is the only sport where you can lose 6-0, 6-1, 6-2 and still enjoy yourself. As long as the sweet scent of victory is in the air, you'll want to keep playing. You'll play "revenge" games until you're blue in the face and can't draw breath because you *know* you can do it. All it will take is one more match to come back and win. It doesn't matter how good the other team is, there's always a chance to win. At least, that's what you tell yourself.

The majority of players feel it's their game. The draw of this sport is unique because it's fun from the very first time you step behind the glass. Players come from squash, tennis, ping pong, and a variety of other racket sports, and immediately feel at home. People who've never before held a racket quickly discover a feel for the game. It's friendly to anyone at any skill level because it's easy to learn yet difficult to master. You always feel you're learning something, but never feel that you're out of the running and unable to win a point.

Anyone can play and learn tactics early on. If it's not already obvious, I love padel for this very reason. Tactics are introduced early in the learning process, which is unusual for a sport in that you don't need a sound understanding of the technique before getting tactics involved. Beginners quickly understand the need for getting their opponents back from the net and discover how effective and important the lob is. Simple tactics come into play very early while advanced tactics take years to master and implement effectively.

In tennis you need a half a dozen lessons before you can even serve. Because the technique for various tennis shots is so complicated, it's hard for a beginner to jump onto the court and have fun right away. This is not the case with padel and its extreme accessibility is why I love the sport. There's no such thing as the perfect sport. Right? Maybe... Maybe not.

Padel also breeds one of the most sociable environments of any sport. Since you almost always play with four people, there's a built-in game mechanic calling for a drink after the game. In tennis, it's more often you'll play a few games against a partner and then head home or run to the next training session. Padel pits you against opponents in close proximity and forces you to work extremely closely with a partner. Padel creates close-knit communities wherever a court pops up.

People of all different personalities, body types, and skill levels take to the court and end up loving padel. It's one of the fastest growing sports of the last decade with millions of players worldwide.[1] Unlike tennis and squash, padel is only going to grow more popular as more people discover it. It's growing so fast internationally because it's easy to learn from a technical perspective, and mentally challenging from a tactical perspective.

> *Padel mostly attracts like-minded people...it is a very network-friendly sport both on and off the court.* —Magnus Ballchand, Stockholm

I've given you insights into my padel journey, prepped you to start thinking about your own reasons for playing, and highlighted many of the reasons padel is here to stay. Now it's time to master your understanding of the game.

Get on the Court

Reflection: *What instincts do you have on the court? Do these instincts need correcting or encouragement?*

Action: *Take a few minutes and write your answers to the "why" questions earlier in this chapter. Gain clarity on what this sport means to you.*

---

1 Padel at the 2023 European Games.
ie2023.pl/en/new/padel-the-fastest-growing-sport-in-the-world.

CHAPTER TWO
Master Your Understanding of the Game

An expert is [someone] who has made all the mistakes which can be made, in a narrow field.

—Niels Bohr

Understanding padel to a greater degree will launch you into the next-level tier. I've seen players come into the padel court strong and aggressive only to leave feeling humbled (and a bit humiliated) when a team slowly wears them down. As long as you have a good attitude, you'll be okay. Take your defeats in turn and learn from the losses that come your way. Above all, have fun and take your learning in stride. Let's master some of the basic fundamentals of padel.

This Is When You Should Begin Lessons (Hint: It's Now!)

You should take lessons right away, it's that simple. Lessons are important no matter what stage of the journey you're on. The earlier you begin, the better off you'll be.

If you want to learn a new language, some experts recommend immersing yourself in a new culture. This might be an extremely effective way to learn a language, but you probably wouldn't enjoy it as you struggle to order a sandwich or get lost after you took the wrong bus. Padel is unique in that learning on court is both exhilarating and a great way to start.

It's at this stage during your momentous discovery that you *should* take lessons. The problem is you don't know *how* much padel is going to be a part of your life, so you don't know whether or not you want to make any sort of commitment. It's tough to spend time and money on lessons if you don't really know how much you like the sport. But I bet there is likely already an inkling you want to go further. Even if it's just to beat your friends or to improve at something, it's worth it to get lessons of some sort, whether that's in person or with an online coach. Whether you've come from racket sports, other sports, or no sports, it's vital to receive in-person instruction to adjust and match your technique to best practices.

If you're missing specific techniques you could be hurting your chances of maximising your game over the long term. You can certainly figure it all out yourself, but this can lead to ineffective and inefficient use of energy, potential injuries, and hitting an early plateau. The earlier you take lessons the better because your coach will be able to correct movement patterns and improve your technique or form before it becomes too ingrained in your subconscious. Players often tell me they don't need to practise racket preparation yet, almost without fail, the player will have his/her racket down by their side and then take a mad swipe at the ball as it comes to them faster than they expected. Everyone has areas of their game they could improve, even players at the World Padel Tour level.

Get lessons to solve potential issues as early as possible so bad habits won't hold you up later. Get started on the right foot. Now is the best time to begin, wherever you might be on your padel journey. Get the basics right and your level will soar. If you're afraid of using the glass (I see you, tennis players!), prefer to stay at the back and defend (yes, that's you, squash players!), or just keep losing your matches and you don't know why, start with one lesson and see how it goes for you. One hour with an experienced trainer might help you more than you expect.

Tips to Quickly Master Padel When You Come from Other Racket Sports

Padel players often come from tennis or squash. They are similar sports, and padel courts are likely at the clubs where people also play tennis and squash. Problems emerge when players try to play padel using similar tactics and strategies. It doesn't work. Tennis and squash players eventually make for excellent padel players, provided they know what pitfalls to avoid.

At first, squash players do well from the back and defend with ease. Tennis players are usually strong at the net and have a powerful and accurate smash, and they do well in the beginning stages because their opponents don't yet know how to deal with hard and flat smashes. But as they progress in level, their opponents quickly see their weaknesses and they inevitably lose momentum.

Here's what to look out for if you've come from either tennis or squash OR want to know what weaknesses to look for in these types of opponents.

Squash:

Padel is more about placing the ball, lobbing your opponents, hitting angles, and trying to tactically get an advantage in the point. You do this in squash, but when you're at the back of the court in squash you can hit with a lot more power because the ball doesn't need to bounce on the other side of a net; it goes directly into the wall and comes back to the corners of the court. You hit a lot harder in squash than you can in padel.

Consider the preparation of the swing. When the ball comes off the wall towards the squash player, they're moving and preparing as the ball is coming towards them, as opposed to padel where the preparation is early before the ball reaches their side of the net. So, the squash player will move across with the racket above the hand behind and away from the body to generate a huge amount of racket head speed. With the addition of the snap of the wrist on the contact, they hit the ball at much faster speeds, and this is problematic if not corrected.

Padel is more about controlling placement and putting your opponents out of position to try and take advantage in the point. Most of the time your contact will be closer to the body allowing you more control of the ball. Because you don't need to generate a fast racket head speed, you shouldn't need to use your wrist in padel as you would in squash. Keep your forearm and wrist nice and strong on your contact to generate a much more consistent shot.

Tennis:

Like me, many players come to the padel court from tennis. I played college tennis, then I played and coached on the tour. When I finally made the move to padel, it took me quite a while to get used to a few areas of the court. I just didn't know what to focus on in the beginning. Tennis players love how much of the game is played at the net, and they take pride in intimidating other players with their overhead smashes and aggressive volleys.

Whether your tennis background is recreational or competitive, these tips are designed to help tennis players improve their padel straight away:

1. Use the walls: Don't be afraid of using the walls. This sounds obvious, but I was constantly half volleying and blocking the ball before the glass because I just didn't have confidence to let it bounce. It's essential to get used to allowing the ball to bounce off the glass. As a guideline, let any ball that lands past the service line bounce off the back glass. It buys you time and ensures you can be more directed with your shot instead of purely reactive. Get through the difficult period and you'll eventually get comfortable with the glass and therefore play better at the back of the court (See image 1).

2. Forget power: Aggressive groundstrokes and attacking volleys and smashes aren't the most important part of the game. If you hit past your opponents in tennis it's a winner, but here they can use the glass and possibly attack you right back. Your opponents can come closer to your side of the court and will be in their net position. So you almost give them an advantage if you hit harder and the ball bounces up and high. Choose the right times to be powerful, but the rest of the time be sensible, strategic, and play with control.

3. Play as a pair: When I first started playing, I was so intent on hitting and then moving forward up the court that I didn't really think about what position that put my partner in. So, if I'm rushing up to net and my partner isn't aware of it, or if I do it at the wrong time, then he's also out of position leaving a big gap down the middle. Come forward and move backwards together (See image 2).

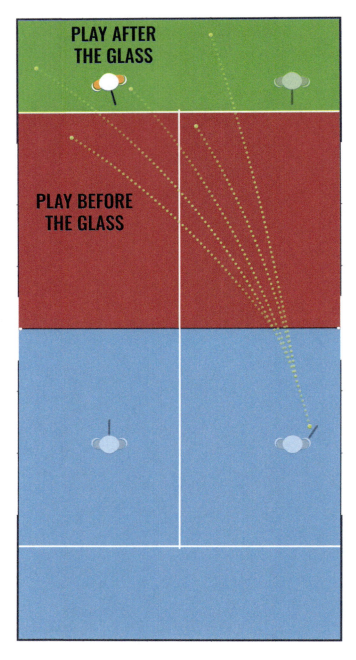

Image 1: When to play before/after the glass.

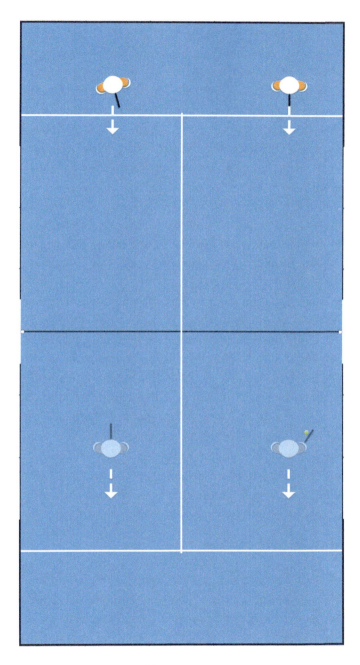

Image 2: How to move as a pair.

The Objective of the Point

The most basic tactic anyone coming to padel needs to know is how to go about winning a point. Write this in your journal as a simple reminder: Win from the net, play it safe while in the back. The primary objective is to make your opponents miss, enabling you to win the point. While winning the point from the back can happen, at higher levels it won't work. Your goal, when you're in the back of the court, is to gain the net. Once you gain the net, you then go about slowly setting yourself up to finish the point from a position of strength.

The goal is to get yourself into a good position where you could potentially win the point but, at the same time, reduce your chances of making an error. Draw your opponents into poor positioning with consistent high-percentage shots, while at the same time strategically positioning yourself to finish the point.

The net is the place you want to be. If you're nervous about being in the front or you're more comfortable in the back, that's okay, but you will ultimately struggle to win points until you overcome this fear. If you and your partner are at net, you're closer to your opponent's court and your ability to aggressively hit down on the ball increases. Force your opponents to retreat to the back and eventually you'll get an easy ball to put away.

Gaining the net position is your sub-goal and the first object for your team to tackle. If you're just starting out, consider it a win each time you push your opponents back and you take the net position. Once you have the net, your goal is to hold it until you are able to hit a winner or your opponents make a mistake. Only surrender the net on a good lob, and when this happens, renew your mission to take the net.

Positioning Is Everything

New players learn how important positioning is in padel. Often, this comes in the form of a skilled opponent spotting your weakness in positioning and crushing you with it until you finally adjust or walk off the court in distress. Positioning is one of the most important facets of the game. If you know how to be in the right place at the right time, you can give even higher-level players a run for their money.

Eventually, as you progress, you'll master setup volleys to move your opponents out of position before you finish them off. This is an advanced strategy and we won't get into it now, but expert padel players are great at positioning. If you play against someone who is always at the right place at the right time it's because they've likely mastered positioning fundamentals. Don't skimp on your knowledge of proper padel positioning.

Positioning begins with where to stand. I know this is extremely basic and you might be thinking, *Duh, Sandy! Let's get to the good stuff!* But I share this because I've seen higher-level players who can kicksmash the ball out of the court get beaten because they aren't aware of their positioning.

Where you stand to start the point depends on who is serving:

1. **You're serving:** Stand behind the line and serve to the diagonal box. Serve, and then immediately sprint to the front. Finish your action and sprint to the front court position. Don't watch the ball, don't stand around. Immediately move to the net position. Serving is an advantage you must utilise! (Image 3).

2. **Your partner is serving:** You're at the net in line with this second post and one step in front (Image 4). If your partner hits a good serve, step forward and be aggressive. If your partner hits a weaker serve and you see that your opponents are going to lob, take one step back and be ready for that lob. This is the position you want to be in as your neutral position from which you can move in either direction.

3. **You're returning the serve:** At the back of the court, you'll be behind the service line lined up one step back from the separation between the first and second panels of glass (Image 5).

4. **Your partner is returning the serve:** Take one step closer to their side to the centre and watch the ball (Image 6). It's your call whether the ball is in or out which allows your partner to focus solely on hitting the ball back. Once they hit their return, move back to your starting position in the back and prepare.

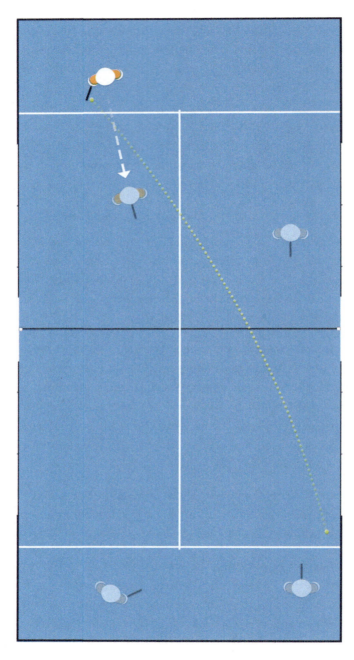

Image 3: Where to move after serving.

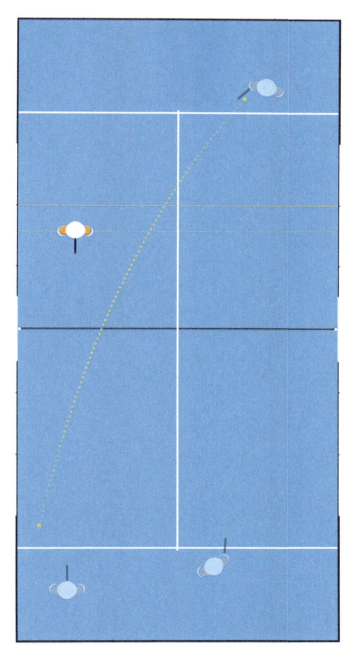

Image 4: Where to stand while your partner is serving.

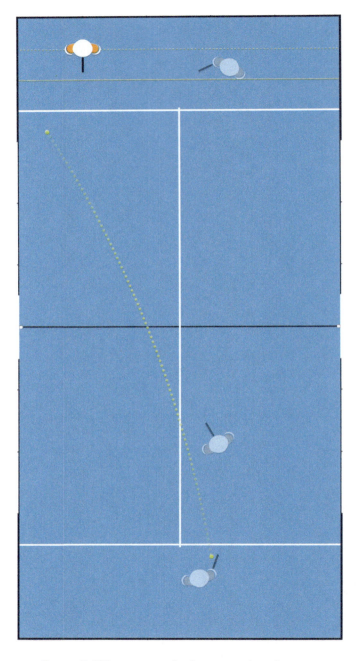

Image 5: Where to stand when returning the serve.

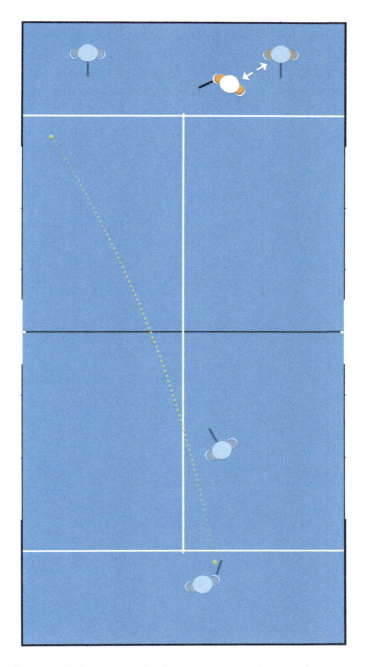

Image 6: Where to stand when your partner is returning serve.

Beyond the basic starting points, you are either going to be in the front of the court at net or in the back of the court. (Image 7) When you're at the net, line yourself up with the second fence post and then take one small step forward. In the back, the position you want to be in is the same as if you were returning your serve (behind the service line lined up with the separation between the first and second panels of glass).

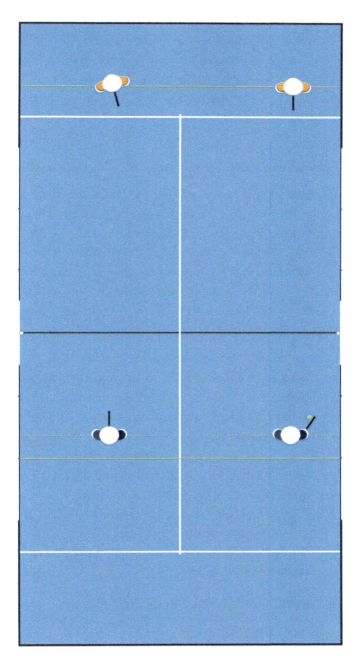

Image 7: Front and back positioning.

If you're not in a good position you're never going to be able to finish the point. Stand too close to the net and you're an easy target for a lob or a fast shot to the body. Find yourself in no man's land (which we will cover later in this chapter) and good players will aim their shots right at your feet. Stray too far to one side in the back and you'll leave the other side open. Stick too close to the back wall and a drop shot could easily take you out.

The two most common mistakes people make with their positioning:

1. **Too far back:** Players commonly get too far back in the court after taking the net, even after starting in a good position. They're too far back in the court to be attacking from the net position, and they leave a big gap in front of them for their opponent to easily hit down to their feet. And they're picking the ball up around their feet, making it easy for the opponent to take the net and attack them. If you fall back you have to pick the ball up from around your feet with a half volley making it harder to be accurate.

2. **Too close** to the net: Sometimes players start too close when their partner is serving, or they hit a few balls, get excited, and then they get too close hoping to quickly finish the point. Instead, they leave a huge space behind them that they can get lobbed in, and you can immediately lose the net from an easy lob.

The best approach is to make a quick decision and stick with it. Choose whether you want to be in the front or back at any given moment. If you're falling back but want to keep the net, hit the ball slowly and then run forward to the standard net position. If you and your partner somehow get separated, pick the right ball (meaning a high ball that gives you time to move) and sidestep backwards or forwards to line up with your partner.

No Man's Land: Bad for You, Good for Them

No man's land is the place where most beginner players never think they are, but often find themselves at the end of the point. (Image 8) It's the area in the middle of the court halfway from the front to the back, between the service line and the second post. We call it no man's land for beginners and intermediates, while at the advanced stage, players find themselves transitioning through it as needed. Sometimes I tell my students they're stuck in no man's land, and I can tell by the looks on their faces that they don't believe me. It's not until I force them to stay in no man's land to play out the rest of the point that they begin to see how much of a disadvantage this positioning can be. If you're stuck in this middle area you're a bit too far back to hit a good effective volley, and you're too far forward to be able to hit a comfortable ground stroke.

Image 8: No man's land.

It's perfectly normal to move through this area to hit a ball if needed. For example, if your opponents hit a lob in an attempt to take the net, and you come back to hit a defensive smash or a bandeja, you're moving through no man's land. Just make sure you retake the net position and don't stop where you hit the ball. Don't stand around in no man's land waiting for the next ball. Either move back in a defensive position in the back of the court or retake the net.

If you're playing against someone standing in this position, and you feel like it's difficult to lob them because there's not a lot of space, play down to their feet. If you play down to their feet, you'll force them to lunge forward and hit a volley closer to the net or back up to play a half volley (we will cover this shot, called the *chiquita,* in chapter 8). Either way, you're getting them to hit the ball in an upward direction meaning that if you're fast enough, you can come forward and hit a more aggressive volley.

The best kept secret of basic court positioning is to become more aware, at all times, of your position on the court. Practise awareness of no man's land by stopping exactly where you are at the end of a rally and look down. You might find yourself in the dead centre of no man's land having no idea how you got there. Increase awareness during your next game by stopping right when the point ends and seeing where you ended. Be hyper aware of your court position and focus on either moving forward to the net or backward.

Move with Your Partner

"Just follow me."

I've heard seasoned players give this simple advice to their newbie partners who don't know where to position themselves on the court. If you're ever not sure where to go on the court, and you happen to be playing with someone who has great court awareness, just follow them. Match their movements and do what they do.

Padel is a team sport; communicating with your partner is crucial.

Make sure you're at the net with your partner or in the back together. If you're both at net together there are smaller gaps in the court. If one of you is at the back and one's at the net, then you open up a big gap in the court. Make sure you move up to the net together when you hit a lob or a chiquita. If your opponents lob you, go back together. Sticking with your partner is a vital part of the game.

During the serve (which at stage one is just focusing on getting it in to begin the point) it's very important to serve and volley. This means that once you serve you join your partner at net to capitalise on the server's advantage of having your opponents starting at the back. If you serve and go straight into that net position, you're already in an advantageous place. Remember, you and your partner have two objectives: A) to keep the net and B) to force your opponents to hit a weaker ball you might be able to finish.

It's difficult to put partner movement into practice, but the key, at first, is not making any sudden movements or rushes. Be unpredictable to your opponents and predictable to your partner. Don't hit a weak return and then immediately sprint to net, because that's obviously very high risk and your partner might follow. The two players at net can easily hit the ball down and put you in a difficult position. Learn to safely play yourself into the point.

Shot Preparation: Ready, Read, React!

Prepare as soon as possible for every shot. I'm proud to sound like a broken record when telling players to prepare early. The common theme of learning any shot in padel is early preparation. Get into the right position with your entire body ready to strike. The sooner you move your body into the right position, the easier it will be to focus on the ball and where it's going.

Expect every ball to come to you and always be prepared. All players up to the advanced level still make this mistake from time to time. If your shot preparation is non-existent and you don't get back early enough by moving fast into position and with your racket in the right spot, your game will suffer. It's really important you get this right when learning the basics because it will prepare you for more complicated techniques later on.

Do you think shot preparation is a problem for you? If so, how do you plan to fix this? Most of my students don't realise it's a problem until I show them proof via video. They are adamant they're doing it right until they watch the video. They say, "Wow! I had NO idea I was dropping my racket to the floor when at the net!"

Practice shot preparation by repeating to yourself: Ready, read, react. Ready, read, react. Ready, read, react.

1. **Ready:** Stand over your toes moving forward with the racket vertical at net (and more horizontal in the back). Be alert and expect the ball to come to you, even if your partner is getting most of the action. You never know when the other team will change direction and suddenly hit a hard ball your way. Not having the racket up and ready and sitting back on your heels is a common mistake we see. Every time your opponents hit, expect the ball to come to you.

2. **Read:** Once you're in a good ready position, you're reading three main areas:

   a. **The game situation:** Determine what's happening on the court, who's attacking, who's defending, and whether you need to move forward or back.

   b. **Your opponents:** Read how your opponents are hitting the ball. What types of shots are they going to hit? Are they going to attack the ball or are they going to have to scoop it and defend?

   c. **Analyse the oncoming ball.** Think: Am I going to have an easy backhand or should I prepare for a difficult corner shot? Is it coming fast or slow, deep or short? Once you practise, you'll be able to tell straight off their racket if it's going to come towards your forehand or your backhand. Immediately get the racket back in the correct position.

3. **React:** As soon as your opponent goes to hit and you're reading their body shape, that's when you split step. The split step is done in the blink of an eye on faster shots but always do it first before moving. React to where the ball is going to end up and prepare accordingly.

If you want to know if this is something that you need to work on, the best thing you can do is watch one of your own matches. Get someone to record video (or set up your phone on a tripod) when you're playing so you can see your preparation. I can't stress the importance of the shot preparation enough. If you improve in this important area of padel it will be much easier to learn even more difficult techniques as you elevate your level.

Get on the Court

Reflection: *What about padel still doesn't make sense? Could you ask a coach or advanced player for help in our online community?*

Action: *Practise ready, read, react. In your next warm up, take five minutes with your partner and practise by saying out loud which shot they are hitting (forehand, backhand), the depth of the shot (short, long), and then speed (fast, slow). For example, you could say something like, "forehand, long, fast" or "backhand, short, slow." Then, in the match, closely watch your opponents and aim to improve your prediction on what shot they are about to hit.*

CHAPTER THREE
Skills for a Solid Foundation

Start where you are. Use what you have. Do what you can.

—Arthur Ashe, American tennis player

Work from a stable foundation and you will win more matches. The first set of padel skills will start you out on the right foot. Learning these will springboard you into the next stage. For each technique or tactic below, take time to practise on the court because the best way to learn is to try it out yourself.

All About the Grip

The continental grip is *the* grip for padel. It's the only grip you need to know and the only one you should use when you begin. This grip allows the most mobility in the wrist, meaning you can change the angle of the racket face and therefore hit different spins on the ball. Check your grip now. Pick up your racket and pretend you're swinging it like a hammer down at a nail. This is the grip you need for every shot. It's also called the chopping or shaking hands grip because it's a similar type of action.

The continental grip gives you the versatility needed to make every shot in padel: forehand, backhand, volley, bandeja, etc. Many people come to the padel court either from tennis or a different background and they're used to using a different grip or slipping into multiple different types of grips depending on the shot. When you're learning, it's okay to have a slight variation. If you need to do so to feel comfortable you can move ever so slightly to a forehand grip, and ever so slightly shift to the backhand grip.

Here are a few pointers when it comes to holding your racket:

- Don't hold the racket too tightly nor too loosely. When you hit the ball, give the racket a firm squeeze, but otherwise hold the racket with a medium-firm grip. That way, the racquet head doesn't wobble and you can keep control of the ball. The rest of the time between shots, keep your hand relaxed on the grip.

- If you're one of those players who wants to have the grip ever so slightly round from continental you can do so, but only from the back of the court. If you're from tennis, it's difficult to go from an extreme grip like the semi-western to the continental, so it will take practice over the course of several matches to feel comfortable.

- At the net, always be ready to block incoming balls with your racket up and your hand ready to squeeze as you swing and make contact.

- Always hold the throat of the racket with your other hand to assist in your preparation.

If you're still uncomfortable, improve your continental grip in a controlled environment. Take your time to make the adjustment. If you're trying to correct it in a match, it will be difficult because you'll be focused on the points, the score, tactics, and what's actually happening in the game! In between game days, find a wall and turn yourself side on. Practise hitting the ball while in your living room (Just don't break anything!). Gain confidence before you step on the court.

Ready Position

You've got the right grip on the racket, now it's time to master the ready position. If you're at the back of the court, stand with your feet shoulder-width apart and slightly bent, head up, racket pointing downward, and with your non-dominant hand on the throat of the racket. At net, you'll be in a similar position as the back except your racket will be up high in front of your chin ready for the ball to come high.

The ready position is a key part of preparation. Without it, players are often late to hit the ball.

The ready position is important in the back of court, but even more vital in the front. I've seen countless players miss balls (or get hit with a smash) because they didn't have the racket up and prepared. As the speed of your padel games intensifies, make sure you start in the ready position and return every time the ball crosses the net.

Split Step

Players who don't start with lessons often miss the split step, and it affects their readiness and reaction times. As soon as your opponent contacts the ball, bounce on the toes. This fires your calf muscles and gets your legs ready to move toward the ball. The split step is one of the basic building blocks to your padel foundation. It's the start of all your movement around the court, whether you're at the net or in the back.

While you're waiting for the ball, stay on your toes and prepare for the ball to go anywhere. If your heels are down when your opponent hits the ball, it's difficult to react accordingly. If you know which direction the ball is coming, you're going to end up pivoting in addition to the bounce of your feet so the movement will increase in speed. If you're not sure where the ball is going, split step, bounce on your toes, and then move straight away as soon as you know.

If you're new to padel, it can be quite difficult to anticipate where the ball is going to end up, but the split step gives you a chance. Once you bounce with the split step, continue to take little steps on your toes while moving into the right position. Don't just bounce and then put your heels down because then it's going to be very difficult for you to generate movement. Once you hit the ball, rapidly return to your position in either the back of the court or the net and reassume the ready position.

When you're learning the game, you can't have too much footwork. Your feet should be sore and tired after each of your matches because you kept moving the whole time! If you watch Roger Federer, you'll see how graceful he is with his movement around the tennis court. When he was a kid and he was learning the game, he had loads of little footwork movements and got himself to a level where he could judge each ball perfectly. Players in the World Padel Tour also know exactly where the ball is going to end up.

Forehand Groundstroke

Learning the basic forehand is a great starting point to be able to rally.

There are several technical elements to consider when hitting the forehand from the back of the court. For stage one, the key is to just get the ball in to continue the rally. Your goal is *not* to hit a winner from the back of the court, which is drastically different from tennis. Yes, there are times when you are able to hit the angles or play into an area you've moved your opponent away from, but most of the time your only goal from the back, at this stage (we'll cover advanced shots like the bajada later on), is to hit the ball over the net and make it difficult for your opponents to attack.

The forehand groundstroke is one of the most basic shots you will learn in padel, yet it's the shot where players get in trouble for trying to do too much. Especially if you come from tennis, your first instinct will tell you to hit hard to get the ball past your opponents. Instead, win padel games by playing soft to slow things down and prolonging the rally.

Here are the three most common mistakes players make with the forehand. Don't get too bogged down in the details (we're only at stage one!) but consider which of these issues you struggle with:

1. **Trying to hit too much spin on the ball**. Players come to the padel court and realise that hitting slice is a good shot because it bounces, hits the glass, and stays down. So what naturally happens is that players try to create so much spin on the ball and end up chopping down on the ball and hitting it into the net or out of the court. You can hit through the ball horizontally with the racket face slightly open to create slice, but you do not need to come chopping down on the ball. Remember, the aim is to keep the shot simple and hit relatively flat. If the ball is above chest height, yes, that is a good time to be a bit more aggressive and have a little bit of slice on it. But you don't need to overwhelm your opponent with spin.

2. **Hitting too close to, or too far from, your body.** This mistake has two parts:

    a. The first part is misjudging the ball and not giving yourself the space to get in the right position. Mastering this comes down to experience, hitting more balls, and practice reading the game.

b. The second part is playing the forehand with an open stance. When you're learning the game, get into the habit of turning your body while keeping the racket to the side using compact swings and moving with the ball. This is particularly important if the ball bounces off the back glass because you'll need to read where the ball is going in order to prepare and react accordingly.

3. **Hitting too hard.** The forehand is usually the most comfortable shot for players which leads to more errors. Players either hit the ball so hard that they lose control, or their shot direction becomes too predictable for their opponents. The forehand is a great opportunity to change the speed of the ball to keep your opponents on their toes. Keep your technique simple so you're in a good position to hit the ball with good variation.

Avoid these errors by taking your time and not doing too much with the ball from the back of the court.

Backhand Groundstroke

To get into the right stance for the backhand, imagine you're holding something in your left hand, and you need to put your keys in your left pocket with your right hand. Move your feet into a side-on position to follow the shoulder turn. Start with the racket down low with a nice bend in your knees and then shuffle with your feet into hitting a flat backhand.

Bend your elbow slightly too, giving you flexibility to turn your wrist. If your elbow is really straight from back, it's difficult to flatten your wrist and you end up kind of jabbing at the ball. Your wrist action is quite an important aspect of the backhand technique. Many players try to hit flat by bending their wrist, but the problem with this is a bent wrist doesn't provide the same strength as a straight wrist, and it's very difficult to time your swing to get it just right. Instead, lead ever so slightly with your elbow so that, in this position, you actually come through, and the elbow is ever so slightly in front of the racket.

There are going to be times when the ball goes into the corner and you might have to lunge for a difficult ball. But if it's on a normal ball, be in a neutral stance where you can draw a straight line from your left foot to your right foot. As you swing, resist the urge to step across. If you step across, you end up twisting, and you really cut down your shot options. From there, you can't get your body momentum into the ball.

Two of the most common errors we see on the backhand side are:

1. **A high takeback:** If players take their racket back too high, they end up chopping down at the ball. They miss hitting through the ball with power. Keep the racket low at the height of where you are going to hit the ball. To practise, point the end of your racket to the ground and be conscious of when you might be taking your racket back too high.

2. **Not moving forward to the ball:** If the ball comes right to the player, they have a nice stroke. But if the ball goes shorter, they don't move up to the ball and they end up contacting the ball way in front, increasing their risk of making a mistake.

In summary, make sure you're in a balanced, stable position. Swing through the ball with a horizontal swing to make contact just in front of your hip. The hands start together on the racket from the back position, but they release during the swing so you finish open. Make small adjustments and take little steps to get into a good balanced position before you swing through to contact.

The backhand groundstroke is not an easy shot to get right. It takes quite a lot of practice to feel comfortable doing it. Coming from tennis, it took me a long while to get this shot right, but now it's probably my favourite shot from the back of the court.

Continue to work on the fundamentals of the game and you will accelerate your learning, have more fun, and even start to beat your friends.

Get on the Court

Reflection: *What is one basic padel technique you have yet to master? Even if you're well beyond the basics, maybe you tend to avoid the backhand, get lazy with the split step when you start to get tired, or make too many errors with your forehand because you are trying to be too fancy.*

Action: *We challenge you to film your forehand and backhand, even if you are hitting against the back wall on your own. Practise perfect textbook technique and send it to us in the community. We will give you some tips if it's not perfect ;).*

CHAPTER FOUR
Ramping Up Your Intensity and Frequency of Play

Just believe in yourself. Even if you don't, pretend that you do, and, at some point, you will.

—Venus Williams

I see you, padel lover. You're reading this book, but your mind is really elsewhere. You're distracted by the thought of your next match. Take a deep breath. It will be here before you know it. For now, let's talk about how to equip yourself for the long-haul of enjoying padel for years to come beyond just the next game.

The passion one finds for padel is unique among all sports. It's a powerful force that grips you the moment you buy your first racket and it only intensifies with time. I've seen kids pick up the game and become obsessed, and older men and women in their sixties and seventies have discovered an intense love for the sport with their only regret being that they didn't find it sooner! It's not an overstatement to say this sport changes lives.

After the initial excitement of playing padel for the first time in a tournament setting, I began to enjoy the sport more and more, especially when I started coaching. Having played tennis for more than twenty years, I never expected to find a new sport and enjoy it so much. More than anything, the tactics brought me in. It's what brings in many players. I was pleasantly surprised at the deep level of tactics I could learn as a player and then impart to students as a coach.

With each student I taught, I shared tactics and strategies to improve their game. With tennis, I only had strategic conversations with players at the highest level. With padel, one can easily understand and implement strategy from the get-go. This is exciting because it gave me hope as a coach that just about anyone who came and trained with me would leave feeling the session boosted their game. They felt as if they already had a chance to improve, which meant I was doing my job as a coach.

This stage of the padel journey is the most precarious because you're likely to start playing padel all the time without even thinking about it. Sure, your arm is starting to hurt, your focus is shifting away from other responsibilities, and your thoughts always seem to be drifting back to padel, but it's all good. Right? Maybe. Maybe not.

As long as you're sensible about your journey, you're golden. If your arm hurts, rest it for a few days. Tennis (padel) elbow is a real problem and not something to play around with. If your love of padel is pulling your focus away from your primary responsibilities, it might be time to take extended time off, however painful that might be.

Without thinking about it, many people start making mistakes and/or hurt themselves. They don't play the game correctly. They buy the wrong shoes, use the wrong racket, play with the wrong people and, sometimes, play the wrong amount. It's not their fault. They don't know any better, but I hate to see the light of a potential future in padel snuffed out early just because of an uneducated or hasty decision.

Regardless of what anyone may tell you, you don't need to spend an arm and a leg to get started with padel. You don't need a top-of-the-line racket, £200 shoes, or fancy padel clothes. What you need is to give your body time, to know your level, and to invest in equipment that matches your current stage. In this chapter, we'll discuss strategies for safely ramping up to play the game smart from the start.

> *Padel teaches about positive communication, team building, and it helps to ease mental stress as it is such a strategic game. You forget about daily concerns while you play. Hence, it is a perfect life-balance sport.* —Kaarle Wirta, Tampere, Finland

Start Slow and Build Up

It's incredibly common to play this addictive sport way too much. Luckily for me, my tennis background helped prevent me from sustaining any serious injuries and my body adapted rather quickly. Most new padel players didn't previously play racket sports, so they usually come to padel suddenly and ramp up faster than their body can adapt to the activity. Listen to your body and only play as much as you can handle.

If something hurts, stop. This is the most important lesson I can impart in stage one. Your body needs time to recover. This is the stage where players are at the most risk for injury and, as a consequence, are unable to keep playing this new game they already love. Padel is a sport that uses a variety of muscle groups like the hip, back, core, and legs for movement around the court. The constant strain on your racket arm from hitting the ball three to four hundred times per match, if unmanaged, can also take a toll.

The good news is that the body adjusts over time. Eventually, if you get the right equipment, develop a warmup routine, and figure out recovery strategies that work for you, you can easily play padel four to five times per week with no problem. But if you go from sitting on the couch OR from not having played any type of racket sport, you need to start slowly and see how your body reacts over time.

One of the worst things that can happen is to hurt yourself and become unable to play. Be sensible about your physical limitations so you're not sidelined for months at a time. You might want to start playing seven times per week, but the nagging pain in your elbow is guiding you otherwise. Listen and slow down.

Injuries can happen to anyone. Some are entirely accidental and there's nothing you could have done to prevent it from happening. Players sometimes get hurt no matter what they do as part of their warmups. Accidents notwithstanding, most padel injuries are preventable.

Avoid Overuse Injuries by Playing to Your Physical Level

I've had my fair share of injuries on and off the padel court. I've suffered from back spasms, rolled ankles, and severe plantar fasciitis. And, as you know, I even tore my ACL during an ultimate frisbee game. According to physical therapist (and avid padel player!) Andreas Olesen, players hurt themselves because they spend too much time using specific muscle groups. Hip, back, and knee pain/weakness is the most common problem Andreas encountered in the players he's worked with. Moreso, the long flights and lack of sleep might contribute to these nagging issues high-level players encounter deep in competition season.

Andreas Olesen shared wise advice on our podcast together:[2]

> *But a lot of times it comes back to general injuries with these recreational players. Most of the injuries I see as a physician are overuse injuries. I don't see a lot of acute injuries in padel.*

Prevent injury by only playing as much as you can handle. You probably don't need to play padel six to seven times per week (even if you might want to). New players should be very careful about playing too much too fast, and hurting themselves as a result. Muscles need time to adjust to the repetitive actions required for swinging around a racket. Give your body time to mould itself to what you are asking it to do. Start with just a few padel matches per week. Frequently self-assess by asking:

- How do I feel overall?
- What, if anything, hurts?
- Do I come back after each game groaning in pain?
- And the hardest question… Do I need to take a break?

---

2 "How to Prevent Padel Injuries - With Andreas Olesen - the Padel School Podcast." The Padel School, 12 May 2022, podcast.thepadelschool.com/1007866/10605460. Accessed 5 Jan. 2023.

[My opponents] laugh because they say, 'Here's the guy that always warms up. He's the only one.' Obviously, I laugh about it, but inside I cry. —Andreas Olesen

Before you play, take ten to fifteen minutes to properly warm up. It's best to get specific advice for your level of ability and body type from a qualified professional, but simple movements like squats, jumping jacks, stretches with a band, and extended leg kicks can be really helpful. If you have trouble areas, address those before you get into a competitive game.

Most players will jump on the court cold after having sat all day at work, but this doesn't have to be you. It's better to warm up in almost any capacity than to skip it altogether. Even if others laugh as you do your squats or downward dog stretches, just laugh along with them. You know why you're warming up: You want to stay limber so you can keep playing padel.

The next time you play a match, show up early. Focus primarily on increasing flexibility and mobility in your hips, glutes, and back with a variety of dynamic (active) stretches.

It's also important to develop an after-match routine to aid your body's ability to recover. There are several methods to try:

- **Rest:** Simply stop movement for a few minutes. Breathe in through your nose and out through your mouth. Don't jump right back into work if you can avoid it. Post-exercise recovery is vital for athletes.[3]

- **Ice/heat:** Ice sore muscles and then use heat therapy to relax. Heat was extremely helpful for me and it's important not to underestimate the power of taking a long, hot shower after your match. Ice and heat are both excellent for post-match recovery efforts.[4]

- **Compression:** Compression socks work wonders for sore feet. You can also use specific compression braces for shoulders or elbows. Use an Ace Bandage on other areas as needed.

---

[3] Doherty, Rónán et al. "The Sleep and Recovery Practices of Athletes." Nutrients vol. 13,4 1330. 17 Apr. 2021, doi:10.3390/nu13041330

[4] Petrofsky, Jerrold S et al. "Cold Vs. Heat After Exercise-Is There a Clear Winner for Muscle Soreness." Journal of Strength and Conditioning Research vol. 29,11 (2015): 3245-52. doi:10.1519/JSC.0000000000001127

- **Stretch:** Before your game, perform a variety of dynamic stretches. Afterwards, cool down with static stretches designed to ease muscle tension and fatigue.
- **Self-massage:** For my various injuries, self-massage was a huge boon. I used to put a tennis ball under my back and massage that area after each game to reduce back spasms and pain. For the plantar fasciitis I rolled a golf ball on the sole of my foot every day. This was incredibly painful, but I eventually worked it into my routine and it made a huge difference.
- **Schedule a break:** Say no to the next padel game if needed. Give yourself the time you need to adjust.

Your physical health is extremely important, especially in these early stages. Wherever you are in your padel journey, stop and ask yourself: Does my current physical level match the amount of time I am playing padel every week? If there is a misalignment, follow the above strategies to better position yourself to continue on your padel journey.

Don't Let Arguments Ruin the Game

> *When the last point is done, we are humans. Give your opponent a hug and say, 'great fight,' and that's all.*
> —Novak Djokovic.

As you advance in levels of competition, don't forget the social heart of this sport. Don't let disagreements ruin the convivial atmosphere. The best way to tell if the ball is in or out is to look specifically at how the ball bounces off either the glass or the court. Sometimes the shot is so close it's hard to tell, but you can use the angle and trajectory of the ball as clues to know whether it hit the glass/fence first or the court. The more you play, the more familiar you'll get with calling these types of shots, but as you improve, the speed of the game increases as well, which makes some calls tough to make.

A good rule of thumb is to play close balls if you are able to. If you're in a good ready position and the ball bounces up and you *can* play it, keep the point going. Help foster an atmosphere of good sportsmanship by giving the other team the benefit of the doubt. Padel is more fun when the rally is long, so don't end it prematurely on a close ball; it's not worth it.

If there is ever any doubt on whether a ball is in or out, repeat the point. Even if you just made the world's greatest shot, play the point again if you aren't sure. Don't let a disagreement ruin the good-natured energy of the sport. Be a good sport and play the point again.

> *One man practicing sportsmanship is far better than 50 preaching it.* —Knute Rockne, Notre Dame football coach

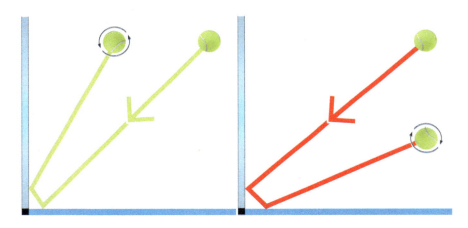

Image 9: How to tell if the ball is in or out

Get on the Court

Reflection: *Do I do a proper warm-up before each game?*

Action: *Before the start of your next match, put a major emphasis on your warm-up. Do dynamic stretches for your legs and arms, jog to the court, or do arm swings from the parking lot to the court. Make use of the time before the game to ensure your body and mind are ready to play at a high level.*

CHAPTER FIVE
Clothing, Basic Equipment, Rackets, and Shoes

The true object of all human life is play.

—G. K. Chesterton

At this stage of your padel journey, you don't necessarily need an indestructible padel bag with space for five rackets, four cans of balls, and three towels. You also don't need to invest in a £350 racket before you even know what you like. Keep your equipment basic, especially when first starting out.

- **Balls:** Make sure you're using actual padel balls. Padel balls are different from tennis balls because they are slightly smaller with a different internal pressure. Replace the balls every three to four games. New balls are much better to play with and help you grow in consistency over time. You can train with older balls for various skills, but it's almost always better to play your match with newer balls.

- **Clothing:** Make sure you have pockets or a place to hold a ball (yes, ladies too!). Make sure you're warm enough (for colder climates) or cool enough (for warmer climates). Clothing for padel doesn't have to be complicated, but it pays to have proper gear for the right situations.

- **Bag:** the most important function of the padel bag is keeping your racket safe. Your racket will be the most expensive piece of equipment you own, so keep it safe with some sort of covering. Otherwise, if you want to get a bag for multiple rackets and to keep your padel stuff together, go for it!
- **Miscellaneous items:** Many padel players like to have various items handy: a wristband/headband, hat, sunglasses, towel, two or three spare overgrips, balls, chalk or magnesium powder if needed to keep your hands dry, extra socks, clean shirt, etc.

Buy equipment to fit your needs. The worst thing you can do is spend extra money on stuff you don't end up using or have to replace. Get what you need, when you need it, and go from there.

What Racket Is Best for Me?

Your racket choice depends on your playstyle and what feels right in your hand. For many players, investing in a higher-quality racket than the one they bought at their local sporting goods store for thirty quid propels them forward. You do not need to spend boat loads of money when you are just beginning the game, but there is a correlation between financial investment and what stage you are at in your padel journey.

With rackets, it's best to start simple. In our interview with professional padel player, coach, and content creator Manu Martin,[5] we learned that just like wine amateurs won't be able to appreciate an expensive bottle, neither will padel newbies understand the intricacies of choosing the most premium racket. If you buy the most expensive racket in the market when you're just starting out, it might be difficult to determine the right racket for you because you don't yet know the ins and outs of your game. You aren't yet able to "taste" the finer qualities of the racket because you are still learning.

It's better to start out with a quality beginner racket to get a feel for how *you* play the game. As you figure out what kind of player you are (left or right side, smash or control, patient or aggressive, etc.), you're able to

---

[5] The Padel School. "Find the Padel Racket for YOU!" YouTube, 23 May 2022, www.youtube.com/watch?v=oNI-n1b8lxM.

choose just the right racket. When starting out with padel, just about any model of racket geared toward beginners will suffice. Look for one that isn't too expensive, has a good balance between control and power, and feels good in your hand from the very first swing.

If you've been playing for a while and you're looking for an upgrade, follow this five-step strategy to find exactly the right racket for you:

1. **Know what you're looking for:** Are you looking for more control or more power? How heavy do you want your racket to be? (350-365 grams for women and 365 to 375 grams for men is a good average.)

2. **Consider the price:** Think about the price and what you would like to invest. £150 is average for an intermediate racket, but prices will vary by location and brand.

3. **Pick two to four rackets that fit your answers to one and two, above:** I know not everyone has a court nearby that also doubles as a padel shop, so it's not always possible to test rackets. Sometimes, clubs have demo rackets they can let you try, or you can ask your friends to borrow theirs for a set or two so you can get a feel for something different.

4. **Compete in a ninety-minute to two-hour match and test each racket:** It's important to test beyond just basic racket feel during a warmup. To truly judge the racket, it's best to compete and give the racket the full treatment and range of shots.

5. **Reflect:** Did any of the rackets stand out? Often, there will be one that feels so solid in your hand that you don't want to give it back to the shop. Otherwise, you could pick the best one, or go back to the drawing board and test two to four more rackets next time.

Don't feel any rush to buy a new racket right away just because you feel you need a replacement. It's better to wait for a great fit than to just buy the first racket you see.

Think about what exactly you need in a racket to match your type of playstyle (or just know you're looking for a beginner's racket), consider your price range, test rackets if possible in a match, and then reflect on what feels best for you. The sport of padel is all about patience, so bring that same approach to finding the perfect racket.

Get the Right Shoes

I try not to recommend a specific model or brand of shoe to students. Instead, I prefer to share three characteristics of what to look for in a good padel shoe:

1. **Flexibility:** When it comes to flexibility of the shoe, you want one that will bend through the sole of the foot, but also that will bend through the toes. In padel, you're pivoting a lot, changing direction, accelerating, and moving your feet to get around the ball, so you need to be able to bend your foot. If you can't bend your toes or your feet, then you end up not being able to engage your calf muscle, making it very difficult to accelerate on the court. Shoes will get more flexible over time, but when you get a new shoe, get something you can test in the shop and see if you can bend it.

2. **Shoe width:** The second characteristic is the width of the shoe. There are some brands that make their shoes a bit narrower and some that make them wider. There are also brands that have a bit of both types to suit both kinds of feet. You are doing a lot of lateral movement in padel, so you want to make sure that it's a comfortable fit around your feet and there's not too much space. The best way to check this is just to try it on and move around. If you feel like your foot is slipping inside the shoe, then it's not the right shoe for you.

3. **Shoe grip:** The third characteristic is the grip, and what you want depends on what type of court you play on the most. If you're playing on a sand court, look for a zigzag (herringbone) pattern on the bottom with a nice deep indentation. If you rub your hand over it, you'll feel it's kind of rough and rigid. That's just the type of feeling you're looking for. If you've got the shoe on and you want to change direction, you'll get a nice grip on the ground so you can move away. If you're playing on a court that isn't sanded, like the

new WPT style courts, all-court tennis shoes actually work quite well because those courts are already quite "grippy". A herringbone sole wrecks my knee on the new WPT surface, so it's wise to have a variety of shoe options at your disposal.

Ultimately, shoe selection comes down to personal preference and testing, but keep the above points in mind for optimal performance. Just like buying any padel equipment, it's important to know what to look for before you start investigating brands. Don't bother getting the latest and the greatest if it won't actually help you excel at padel.

Get on the Court

Reflection: What characteristics do I like in a racket?

Action: List these characteristics and conduct your own research to see which models fit that. If you're looking for a new racket, test a few rackets at your local club to try to find the perfect fit.

CHAPTER SIX
Basic Improvements You Must Make Before You Advance

Some may have more talent than you, but there is no excuse for anyone working harder than you do.

—John Tavares, professional ice hockey player

It's time to move beyond celebrating every time you hit the ball over the net. At this stage, you're ready to master the padel serve, make your opponents fear your intimidating net play, get more comfortable with the glass, uncover the most versatile shot in padel (the lob), and even start practising the more challenging bandeja. You're ready to begin a steady march toward improvement. It's not easy to learn new techniques, and it's incredibly difficult to put what you learn into a match. It's one thing to practise the bandeja with a coach for an hour, but when you're forced to move your feet, prepare, and then hit the ball correctly during a match, the difficulty is increased tenfold.

The best advice I can give you is to take your time and be patient with yourself. Pick one or two of the items in this chapter and get on the court and practise. In The Padel School courses, I always stress the importance of not overwhelming yourself with too much information. Your learning journey might feel like it's taking a while, but incremental progress is the best way to learn the skills without the danger of missing important milestones.

All players at any level need to hear this: You don't have to win all of your matches right away. In fact, some of the best learning comes on the heels of losing a match. I urge you to leave any preconceived notions of what progress is supposed to look like at the door and, instead, ensure your foundation is as strong as possible. Take any losses in stride, learn something each time, and you will improve quicker than you thought possible.

> *Setting specific objectives and consistently working towards them, rather than working sparsely trying to cover everything. [This has been the most effective way to improve my padel game]* —Nikhil Mohindra, Leatherhead, UK

Mastering the Padel Serve

At the professional level, players rarely miss their serve returns. At the beginning and recreational level of your first stage, you can do some real damage with your serve by putting your opponents under pressure right away. Regardless of your current level, it's important to have a consistent serve you can use to start with an advantage in the point. Step up to the line to start the rally in your favour by serving deep and taking the net.

Here is a five-step process for serving like the pros:

1. **Bounce or drop the ball in front and to the side:** Get your bodyweight into the shot. This simple setup allows you to swing freely to the side of your body on the shot. If you're not dropping the ball in front and to the side, it means that you can't fully swing into that ball and get your body weight into the shot.

2. **Take the racket back:** Prepare with the racket head back to the farthest point to ensure maximum follow through. If you don't take the racket all the way back, you can't get a full swing. Start with the racket low and bump the ball up on a short bounce. The power and the swing speed is very different than if the racket starts closer to the ball.

3. **Contact the ball at waist height or just below:** Never contact a low ball around ankle height for the serve. If the ball is too low it has to

go up before it comes down on the other side of the net. A bigger and steeper trajectory on your side means the ball will bounce higher on the other side. If you can contact around waist height, it will still have to go up a little bit over the net, but it will be a lot shallower and, therefore, it will stay lower at the other end which is what you want. If your drop or bounce is too low, you are allowed to repeat the action as long as you don't hit it.

4. **Hit with slice:** Hit a little bit of slice on the ball to keep it low at the other end. You won't see any World Padel Tour players hitting these funky side spins or trying to hit topspin into the corner because they know the most effective serve is flat with a little bit of slice.

5. **Move forward:** Serve and volley after you hit the ball so your team keeps the net. Once you've hit your serve, you should already be moving one or two steps before the ball crosses the net or bounces on the other side of the court. Get into your net position as quickly as possible. Split step as soon as your opponent makes contact. Don't just stand there and watch the ball to see where it's going; instead, practise moving as you serve.

Serving is the only moment you are in complete control of the time on the court, so take your time. Adjust and improve your serve as you learn the game to maximise your starting position on serving points.

A Force at the Net: Learn How to Volley

As we said earlier, the most important part of learning padel is to be an expert at preparation and to always expect the ball to come to you. For the volley, hold the racket slightly farther from the body and more vertical. This way, you're faster to react when the ball comes to you. At the net, you're also closer to your opponents and the ball is going to come faster. Always be ready to block a fast shot with good preparation.

Move the racket back as far as the back shoulder or just slightly farther. If you're hitting a forehand, then you're going to step forward with your left leg. If you're hitting a backhand, step forward with your right leg. (If you're a left-handed player, you'll need to reverse these.) Get your body ready to push into the court with a nice stable base.

When the ball comes, block it by contacting just in front of the body. This is not a full swing, it's just a nice strong block. Keep your forearm and wrist strong, and be prepared to take the power that's come from their shot and rebound it back. The key is to just keep this technique nice and simple, especially when you're learning.

If you're having trouble hitting a strong volley, here are a few reminders that might help:

- **Keep the racket above the height of the hand:** This will keep your wrist and forearm in an optimal position. When the racket head drops below the hand you immediately lose strength and stability of contact. If you're picking up a really low ball this might be necessary, but whenever possible keep the racket above the hand (and bend your legs to get lower).

- **Use the continental grip:** The grip is extremely important for the volley because you don't have time to change the grip depending on which shot is coming your way. You need to be able to react quickly. Keep the continental grip and turn the shoulders every time you strike.

- **Don't stand too close to the net:** Your reaction time will be slower and it will be easier for your opponents to lob you. As a guideline, stand between the first and the second post about two to two and a half metres from the net. This sweet spot will give you the room needed to go forward to be aggressive but won't leave too much space behind you.

- **Don't overcomplicate the backhand volley:** Volleying on your backhand side has the same purpose but the form is slightly different. The key to a good backhand volley is to have a firm forearm and wrist so there's no wobble when you contact.

- **Move your body:** Always remember to move into position before you hit the volley. This is especially important with a low volley because you need to get low with your body while still keeping the racket head above your hand to keep control. What you see a lot of players do, especially when they're learning, is drop the wrist, and then use their wrist to snap at the ball. Instead, move your body into position as soon as possible to avoid this type of last-second jabs at the ball.

The Different Types of Volleys

Responding with the right volley at the correct time will take practice. You will get a huge variation of balls that come over the net and you need to be able to deal with them in different ways. The spectrum of shot types ranges from the reactive block volley all the way to the super slow ball you can pop out the back of the court. Each type of volley presents its own unique challenge:

- **Block volley:** A fast ball at your body will come from a smash by your opponents when they are deep in their court. It will likely put you into a difficult position and you won't have a lot of time to react. Try to get a nice solid contact on the ball and hit it back into the court. You're not trying to do too much with the ball at this point. Your only goal for a block volley is to hit it back to the other side while not giving your opponents an easy ball to finish off.

- **Neutral volley:** The neutral volley occurs when your opponents hit a good ball and you can't necessarily attack it, but you're able to guide it into a position where they can't attack you on the next ball.

- **Standard volley/setup volley:** This is where the ball is coming with medium speed but you have time to react, split step, and push by hitting a nice, medium-aggressive volley with the purpose of setting yourself up to potentially finish on the next ball.

- **Aggressive volley:** Your opponents just hit a weak or soft shot, and you've got time to turn with your body and be aggressive. You're able to have fast racket-head speed through the ball and a nice aggressive shot into the corner. Ideally, your volley is so good that you can win a point on it or at least set up the next shot so you can then finish the point.

There are going to be times when you have to hit a volley in between the volleys listed. For example, you might get a type of ball that leads you to think, *Yes! I can be more aggressive on this ball, but it's coming too fast, and I don't have quite enough time to be super aggressive on it. So I have to hit something in between.*

Discovering the pace of the game at the net is one of the most exciting elements of padel. Learn to predict where the ball is going, react accordingly, and your net game will rapidly improve.

Using the Glass

The glass is your friend, not your enemy. You must get comfortable using the glass because it slows the game down and gives you time to make better shots. If you're from tennis, your instinct might be to either half volley or block every shot that comes your way, but making this a habit will only hurt you in the long run. When balls start coming at you faster and faster it will be much harder to block consistently from the back.

You've got to force yourself to use the glass to build up your confidence with it. And after that, it's going to be a very useful shot in the game. The ball loses speed when it hits the glass so if you get behind it early enough, it's easier for you to get your body weight into the ball. Plus, it's more natural to approach and come forward into the court than to move forward on a half volley or a volley at the back of the court. So if you practise it, you'll be able to put it into a game.

One rule that might help you: If the ball bounces on or behind the line with a bit of speed, let it bounce off the back glass. Unless it's going to bounce slowly and softly, let it bounce off the glass (Refer back to image 1 from chapter two). When learning, you'll have a lot of balls you'll read incorrectly and end up having to lunge for. But unless you experience the glass and build your confidence, you're never going to be able to put it into a match.

As soon as you see the ball is going to bounce deep, prepare your racket and move back early with your feet, and then move forward again to contact the ball in front of you. The same rule applies if the ball is going to hit off of both glasses, which we call a double glass bounce (which we will discuss in depth in chapter 10). If the ball is going with some speed into the corner, allow it to hit the first and second glasses before you hit your shot. There's no point in letting the ball come off one glass and then rushing desperately to try to take it off the second glass. If you give it a bit more time it will come to you and will make for an easier shot. Start practising this shot as early in your game as possible, even if it means you miss a few balls from time to time. It's better to miss a few and improve than to keep making the same mistakes.

Unlocking the Magic of the Lob in Three Steps

The lob is one of the most important yet underutilised shots in padel. A good lob changes the dynamic of the game, increasing your chances of gaining the net and of winning the point. The lob can buy you time, push your opponents back, and help you achieve the primary objective in padel which is to win the net. It's also a great change of pace for the game and can reset the board if your opponents move you and your partner out of position. As you're growing your skills, an effective lob is one of the most useful tools you can learn.

Here's how you can hit an effective lob in three steps:

1. **Take the racket back:** Start in the ready position and prepare like you would for any other shot. Get your racket back and turn to the side with the racket head low and ready to sweep upwards.

2. **Focus on footwork:** Remember the importance of good footwork and setting yourself up for the shot. When you hit the ball, return to ready position either in the front or the back of the court.

3. **Hit with upward motion:** Come up through the bottom of the ball and finish with the racket up high to get the lob to go high and deep. Use your legs to drive the ball upward.

When you master the basics of the lob, you can then activate the more advanced high lob or a fast lob. A fast lob will bounce lower and will give your opponents less time to run back and attack, but it's also more challenging to hit without making a mistake. Use the fast lob if your opponent is sticking too close to the net and you can drive them back. A high lob is best for slowing down the game and regaining the net position. Hit a high lob as high and deep as possible given the limitations of your court to drive your opponents back.

A common pitfall to avoid is choosing the wrong ball to play the lob. If you're pressured and out of position, it's going to be harder to hit the lob exactly where you want it. Wait until it's just in front of you and hit up through the ball. Aim to hit the ball deep into the court past the service line. And if you hit a higher lob it will bounce and stay closer to the glass. If you hit a fast lob that's lower and bounces and comes off the glass then it's easier for the person to attack. A deep lob forces your opponent back, granting you easy access to the net position.

Beginning the Bandeja

The most important detail to remember is the intention behind this shot in padel. It's a defensive shot that buys you time to regain the net. You do this by hitting a slow and controlled ball that stays low at the other end that is hard for your opponent to attack. The bandeja is a shot that is unique to padel that you won't find in any other racket sport. When hitting this shot, the takeback position of your racket is high above your body with your elbow up and the racket held almost horizontally. "Bandeja" means "tray" in Spanish, as the prescribed ready position used to look like that of a server holding a dinner tray. However, in today's faster-paced game, the racket face is less open.

To prepare for this shot, recognize when you are going to use it. As soon as you see it's a lob, like you would do for most smashes, go back into the ready position by immediately turning your shoulders and your hips and prepare by side stepping back into position. Move straight into this position with your racket high above your shoulder with your elbow relatively straight and the racket pointing vertically or tilted slightly to be more open. Move your feet back into the position to keep your momentum forward. Remember, the point of this shot is to regain your net position. If your body weight is going forward, it's going to be much easier for you to keep your momentum forward and keep the net.

In the beginning when you're learning this shot, it's going to feel slightly awkward. Especially if you're from tennis it will feel unnatural to position your body and your racket in such a way. You might find it challenging to contact to the side of the body, at eye level, as opposed to contacting up high as you normally would. If you contact the ball too high, the trajectory of the ball is going to cause it to bounce, hit the glass, and then come up making it easier for the other team to defend or even attack you. If you make contact to the side it's going to be more difficult for them to defend because the ball stays lower and deeper in the court.

One of the best ways to practise the bandeja is to take a bag of balls and just throw them up for yourself to get used to the motion. If you can, record yourself and see what it looks like and adjust from there. With this shot (more than most) the way you feel you're hitting it might not reflect how you're actually hitting it. Watching yourself and your form is a quick way to correct any issues, especially if you're familiar with the theory of the shot. If you hit 100 bandejas with proper form, you're going to have a lot more confidence when it comes to hitting this shot in a match when it counts.

Regardless, don't overthink any of the techniques mentioned above when you're in a match. Use the time in between to change and adjust as needed. Make steady and incremental progress toward your goals of padel domination.

Beyond the Bandeja: Learning the Gancho

The gancho is another defensive overhead to add to your arsenal. Just like the bandeja, it's used to keep your opponents back in the court so you can keep the net. It's not a shot you want to hit hard, because you likely don't have the time, angle, and/or power to be aggressive. The intention here is not to win the point, but to keep the rally going to eventually set up a winner. With the bandeja, you are moving around to the left side of the ball and letting it drop to about head height. This is preferable to the gancho, because it's easier to keep the ball down at the other end. With the gancho, you are looking for a ball that comes to your left side that is difficult to get around in time to hit a clean bandeja. The gancho is especially useful as a means of keeping your net position because it gives you an extra few steps in front that you don't have to run to get behind the ball. And of course, it's always helpful to vary your shot selection so you aren't being too predictable.

The technique for the gancho is to turn your shoulders and lift your arms up like you're preparing for an aggressive smash. Hit the ball over the top of your head with a straighter arm and make sure that you make contact in front of you, slightly down and hitting through the ball with good follow through. Your aim is to hit the fence, side, and/or back glass to make the ball difficult to defend and to keep your opponents in the back. You might see the pros hit this shot down the middle, and that's perfectly fine, but it likely will be very easy for your opponents if they are already in a good position. However, if they are expecting you to kill the ball and instead you hit a soft gancho down the middle, this fake smash could be a winner.

Master each of these basic padel shots to elevate your game to the next level.

Get on the Court

Reflection: *Are there certain shots I find more difficult than others? Is this a technical issue or a decision-making problem?*

Action: *Buy a tripod this week if you don't already own one. Record a video of your overheads and put it in the community so we can take a look and provide immediate feedback. Keep improving!*

Stage Two
Rapid Improvement & Breakthrough

Chapter Seven
Play to Improve

We don't want to tell our dreams, we want to show them.

—Cristiano Ronaldo

Some of my favourite moments in padel were not as a player, but as a coach. Our players, Toby and Mike, registered me as their coach for a weekend FIP tournament in London. I was honoured and vowed to help them as much as possible. It was a beautifully sunny Saturday morning with a crisp edge to the air common with competitions like this one. "I'm here if you need me, but otherwise, I'm happy to hang back and just let you play," I said to Toby before the game.

Toby replied with a smirk, "Come on in if they are putting a beat down on us and it looks like we need help."

With a laugh I responded, "No worries, mate. Let's just see how it goes."

As bad luck would have it, the first set didn't go well at all and they suffered a brutal defeat 6-0. As I watched, I took mental notes of what they could do better. I walked over to the court and brought as much positive energy as I could before putting on my coach's hat to share my thoughts. "Well, as promised, I'm here. How can I help?" I said with as much gusto as I could muster to lessen the pressure and lighten the mood. No one feels good after losing 6-0 and I could tell they both felt a bit down.

"Yeah, that game was a real letdown. What can we do differently? I'm not sure what we can do, they were pressuring us on every shot," said Mike.

"What was your strategy going in?" I asked innocently.

Mike stared back at me and said, "Strategy? What do you mean, strategy? It was our first game against them."

"Ah, I see. It looked like you both switched who you were attacking at random times, but I wasn't sure if there was a method to your madness. Let's start with a framework and you can build from there. Aim to play your lobs down the centre. When you come forward, play setup balls to the middle. When you're at the back, mix between hitting low to their feet and then hitting a lob to the middle on the right ball."

After this extremely simple and straightforward pep talk, they were determined to give the other team a hard fight. They won the second set 7-5 and had great momentum going into the third set, which they ultimately lost because their opponents adjusted to their strategy, but it was a good lesson for both of them in how important it is to come in with a plan and focus on its execution.

Each time you step on the court, whether it be for a friendly game or a pro tournament, come with intentionality and a plan. When all else fails, strategy and tactics are a great way to improve your game at any time.

Reduce Bad Habits in Matches

Maximising your learning and growth during your matches is critical. In tennis, lessons are more frequent with less match play in between. In padel, even if you have lessons once per week, you're likely playing several times in between. You get to learn on the court with trial and error against real opponents who are trying to expose your weaknesses and take advantage to win points. There is nothing like this real-time learning for growth, but the problem comes when you develop "bad" habits that affect your game.

People normally don't become addicted to learning and improving their skills, they become obsessed with beating their friends and enjoying great competition. But you need not focus on winning in order to have fun, improve, and keep the sport interesting. In every match you play, be intentional to work on specific skills. Make learning the primary goal and keep winning as a nice secondary bonus.

As a competitive person, I know how tough it can be to miss a few shots just because you were trying to learn a new technique. It's harder if your partner is competitive as well because you might feel you're letting them down. But just think about how beneficial it will be to your game if both you and your partner learn to consistently hit a bandeja to keep the net. You won't learn this skill without repeated failure first.

Communicate your intention to your partner and tell them you are working on your bandeja and you might miss a few shots here and there. Good partners will smile and nod and be happy you are bent on improving! Have candid discussions with your partner about whether it's more important for you to win or to improve. Likely, they will agree that improvement over the long run is more important, so verbalising your thoughts is good practice as you learn to work with your partner.

To avoid developing too many bad habits, focus on one or two skills/tactics at a time for each match. For your next game, try one of the following challenges:

- Only hit lobs off easy balls… No "defensive lobs" are allowed!
- Be extremely safe from the back of the court by hitting sensibly to the middle.
- Don't focus on "winning" points. Focus on extending the points and forcing your opponent to make the mistakes.
- Challenge your partner to a game within the game. See who can make fewer errors. You can make it more complicated and count each winner against your errors. This is helpful to your personal analysis because you'll notice there are almost always more errors than winners in any given recreational game.

Use your matches to improve by focusing on removing any lingering bad habits within the game. Use your time off the court to target technique and then find ways to implement and improve while you're playing matches.

In-Person and Online Resources

Not everyone has access to great coaching. I completely understand that it may be difficult to find a good coach in your local padelsphere. It's even more difficult to find a coach who's decent at the game, knows advanced strategies, and is equipped to impart their knowledge. It takes time and energy to find the right person you immediately connect with who understands your level and what *you* need in order to improve. So, depending on your unique situation, you may not have access to a great coach.

Learning online at your own pace is excellent for taking ownership of your abilities and to know what you need to work on next. However, you can't just sit and watch videos and hope to improve. You have to actually get out there and practice on a court. For these reasons, I strongly recommend mixing in-person training (even if it's with a training partner) with online resources for best results. Know what you need to improve by learning online, and then find a coach/partner who will help you get to the next level. It takes focused on-the-court practice to see real improvement.

Let's say you want to improve your bandeja. Many people coming from tennis, squash, or table tennis don't have any familiarity with this unique-to-padel shot, so it takes a multi-step process to master it. It's extremely difficult to put this technique into practice without the aid of a coach and a bucket of balls. But if you start out with no idea what a bandeja is, it will take extra time out of your session for your coach to explain what it is and why you need it. Before you train this skill, view online resources to go into the training with a basic familiarity of the concept and purpose of the bandeja, and any other skill you want to learn, to master the technique much faster.

View online resources to enhance your learning between lessons. Find a coach, training partner, or group and record your sessions. Watch the videos and help each other improve. Grow in self-awareness and correct your mistakes. Become an unstoppable force on the padel court.

Help Your Coach Help You

The worst thing you can do at this stage is to start thinking you know more than your coach. Be willing to admit you don't know what you're doing. Don't be the impediment to your own progress.

Let me let you in on a little secret: When players come to me willing to learn and change their way of doing things, I'm more likely to put extra effort in to help them get where they need to go. Of course I want success for all my students, but if you're willing to put in the work, you can almost guarantee your coach will too. I can't tell you how many times I've had players come in with their own ideas of how to do things. This, in and of itself, is perfectly normal. I don't expect my students to have all the right answers! It's my job to set the ship straight, but it's much easier to do so if you show a bit of humility and a willingness to improve.

The problem comes when players nod their heads and agree with what I am saying, but all they're really thinking is, *Nah, I'm going to keep doing it my way.* This is fine, but I wonder why they are getting lessons if they don't want to improve?

Becoming coachable is an art form and takes practice if you aren't inherently good at it, but here are a few quick strategies I recommend every wannabe padel star follow:

- **Listen to your coach:** When on the court, do your best to follow their instructions while putting to bed your own bad habits and preconceived notions.

- **Ask questions if you don't know:** This is the time to learn! Don't be afraid to ask questions. I encourage our coaching staff to prompt students to ask lots of questions to drill down and get as specific in their advice as possible. As a coach, I love questions, and likely your coach will too.

- **Check your ego at the door:** Even on the off chance that your coach is worse at padel than you are, you can still learn from them. Go into your lesson willing to receive new instruction even if it means abandoning the way you used to do things. If you disagree with their stated techniques, ask questions about why they think that approach is better than your alternative.

- **Aim to grow:** Come to lessons fully prepared to improve your padel game. Progress comes when hard work meets desire.

- **Take notes and work on problem areas between lessons:** One last measure of a great student is one who takes notes and works to improve between sessions. Don't keep coming to your sessions making the same mistakes. Use your time in between to improve.

Develop a coachable nature and you will make incredible progress.

Record. Watch. Implement.

Beyond online resources and in-person coaching, it pays to become more keenly aware of your own game and what exactly you need to improve. Recording your games and then watching them with an introspective eye is a great tactic for personal improvement. I mentioned this idea previously, but when you get to this stage it becomes even more valuable to record because you have an advanced understanding of the game. This way, you can reflect on what you're doing well, but also what you need to improve.

> *One needs to interact with reality fast and learn from the feedback loops that it creates. Recording your own games is a great way to do that!* —Ahmed Butt, London

Watching yourself is useful because you can replay it and gain awareness of exactly how your approach works within a match setting. This improved awareness is a skill you will carry over into other areas of padel, making you a better overall player. Instead of being that player who hits ball after ball after ball out of the court exclaiming, "Oh no!" (Or another expletive) forty-five times a match, you'll more quickly correct your own mistakes.

Recording games helps you take account of your own unique abilities and strengths. On the training court, your coach might try to adjust form or technique when you've already discovered another way that works better for you. Become aware of your skill level so you can be selective on the feedback you receive. If your coach is trying to switch your serve mechanic, but you're happy with how it's working for you in the game (and you've seen evidence of this on film), you might not need to change. This awareness will help you know when you should listen and adjust without comment, and also show you when to ask questions about the reasons behind their suggestions for improvement.

To record your games, all you need is one of my favourite equipment purchases: a simple tripod. More than picking the perfect racket, my trusty tripod has helped me level up my game. It means I'm able to watch myself play, share the video with others to get their thoughts and opinions, and then practise specific growth areas.

When we do our online coaching, our players improve fast because they're analysing their matches. We make sure they go beyond just watching our instructional videos to put techniques and tactics into real match practice. Not only are they sharing it with us so we can provide valuable feedback, they are learning to adjust on their own by watching themselves!

Instead of going to a coach and spending an hour hitting balls from a basket (which, of course, is helpful in other ways), our players are getting feedback and notes for improvement on the exact problems keeping them from winning matches. They improve fast because we're able to pinpoint items they need to work on within their game.

Here is how to record a game and create an easily shareable video file:

- Buy a simple tripod. It doesn't need to be anything special, but make sure it extends high enough to get a broad view of the entire court. Forty-two inches should suffice.

- It takes all of forty-five seconds to set up the tripod behind the court with your cell phone. You could use a dedicated video camera to record the games, but the camera on your cell phone should be more than sufficient.

- Download the recording as-is or edit it first. It's very easy to skip around on the video player as needed, but if you're familiar with video-editing software, cut out any dead space such as the warmup to make for an easier-to-use file.

- Watch your video and take notes. Ask yourself a series of questions: What did I do right? What could I improve? Is there any one specific goal I should make for my next match?

- Upload the video directly to YouTube and mark it as "unlisted." This is the easiest way to share the video because all you need to send is a link. Send your video to a few friends and ask for their feedback. In our Padel School community, it's common for players to upload recordings of themselves playing games. Then other members provide helpful and kind feedback to help them improve. This level of direct feedback takes a commitment from players. If you're willing to follow through to record your games and share the results, you're one step ahead.

- Score your game if you aren't afraid of the results! Take note of everyone's errors and winners to see how you stack up compared to your friends. Then compare yourself with your personal results on your next recording to see if you are improving.

This personal empowerment and improved self-awareness will quickly raise your padel level AND will make your in-person coaching sessions more impactful. Instead of asking your coach, "What should we practise today?" tell them what you know you need to work on. Coaches love working with players who understand their faults and actually want to improve and take advice. Learning how to intentionally plan your next steps for growth is vital.

Make it a priority to improve your game on and off the court. The best players take it upon themselves to improve their weak areas and work at it until they make measurable progress. Record yourself during your coaching session and/or your next match. Seeing yourself play is painful at first, but those who record themselves and adjust accordingly see rapid improvement.

Then, on your next lesson, you can admit to your coach that they were right, you weren't hitting the bandeja low enough after all.

Play with Various Types of Players

> *You're the average of the five people you spend the most time with.* —Jim Rohn

Stop playing with the same four people three times per week with winning as the primary goal. Your level will maintain the status quo of the group if you don't mix it up. If you play with only the same people, it will take much longer to improve because you're all making similar mistakes.

If you are involved in various groups and competitions, aim to mix the levels of who you are playing with. This might not always be within your control, but when possible, adjust your opponents accordingly. If you are going for the absolute ideal scenario, this is what I recommend:

- **25% of games against weaker opponents:** Book 25% of your games with players who you know you can beat when you're at your best. It's extremely important to comfortably and consistently beat players who are worse than you. Finesse your way to a win against weaker opponents regardless of their attitude, demeanour, or playstyle. Learn how not to be threatened by the unknown.

- **25% at your level:** When you play against players right at your level you'll be pushed appropriately. These games, if you can find them, are the sweet spot of enjoyment as you head into multiple tiebreakers and/or play for several hours at a time, duking it out as you sweat profusely.

- **50% better players:** It's mostly better to play with better players who will push you to higher heights. Better players expose weaknesses. If you can't defend the corner or don't know how to hit a proper bandeja, they will make you feel it. These kinds of matches are the fastest ways to improve.

A Short Note on Fitness

Your fitness level will determine how far you get with padel. This is not a book about health-and-fitness advice, so I advise you to seek additional information on this subject if you're curious. But I would be remiss if I didn't mention its importance as you continue to improve and head towards competition. At stage two, it's a necessary avenue of consideration as you seek to improve your skill level and dive deeper into this game.

High-level padel players are able to move rapidly around the court with strong glutes and leg muscles. Their cores are strong to keep their balance and avoid injury from the repetitive motion of squatting to return low balls. Their arms are naturally toned to avoid the dreaded tennis elbow and to prevent shoulder injuries stemming from hitting various smashes.

You can be relatively unfit and still do well at padel, so fitness largely depends on how far you want to go and how much you want to improve. Again, this is why determining your *why* for playing padel is so important. If your goal is to just have fun and play a few times per week, then your fitness level may not be overly important. But if you want to start winning high-level competitions, you'll need to be in good enough shape to avoid injury and play long rallies. Just know that the top players in the game do physical training in the gym two to three times as much as they practise on court.

The best advice I can give you on fitness is to make sure to do a proper warmup before each match. An ideal warm up should begin with a few minutes of light aerobic exercise to get your heart pumping and to increase blood flow to the muscles. Follow this with a series of dynamic stretches, targeting the major muscle groups involved in padel, including the shoulders, arms, legs, and especially your core. Arm circles, torso twists, lunges with rotations, and leg swings are excellent exercises to improve mobility and flexibility. Additionally, incorporating specific padel movements, such as side shuffles, forward/backward sprints, and lateral lunges help activate the muscles used during gameplay.

Start with your warmup partner at mid-court and just play softly to each other. Work your way to the back of the court, but don't hit at 100 percent. Stay up on your toes and move around quickly the whole time. When it's your turn to move to the front to hit volleys, gradually increase the intensity of your shots to prepare for the game. Hit a few bandejas, viboras, and a few topspin smashes when you feel ready. This simple warmup process goes a long way towards keeping you healthy, fit, and happy as you continue to enjoy padel.

• •

Get on the Court

Reflection: *What conditioning am I doing off court? Is my physical fitness a hindrance or a strength?*

Action: *Record your next padel game. As you watch it, write down two to three areas for improvement you can tackle during your next lesson, match, or individual training session.*

CHAPTER EIGHT
Reading and Controlling Your Match

I didn't have the same fitness or ability as the other girls, so I had to beat them with my mind.

—Martina Hingis

As you progress in your padel level, you'll notice players who tend to win their matches are well-rounded. They learn to keep their errors down, forcing the other team to hit winners in order to take the game, and they take just enough risk when hitting winners of their own. At almost every level except for the pros, there are far more unforced errors in a game than winners overall. If you can read the game effectively and practise consistency, you'll win more often.

Become a well-rounded player opponents fear by fixing any weaknesses and understanding the game more deeply.

Checkmate: Shot Anticipation and Reading the Game

Winning a game of chess involves painstakingly moving your opponent into a bad position, killing his queen with a trap, and powering forward with your knights until you are finally able to checkmate the king. Winning at padel is strikingly similar. You have to constantly position yourself in defensive and offensive positions to keep the flow of the game moving toward your eventual victory. But you can't win on the first move.

In chess, there are trillions of combinations for how the game might play out.[6] Some might argue that padel (and other sports for that matter) is just as complex as this seemingly simple board game. Nevertheless, there are many things going on within padel and the ways to win are seemingly endless. It's hard to predict everything that is going to happen.

To help break down the possibilities of what can happen every time the ball travels over the net, here are three advanced strategies for reading the game and predicting your opponent's next move:

1. **Predict based on your own shot:** Wherever you hit the ball, your opponents only have a certain number of possible returns. The potential shots they can hit range from likely outcome, to unlikely outcome, to straight up impossible. For example, if you've hit a lob down the middle and the right-side player comes across and plays it with their backhand, there are certain shots that are physically impossible for them to hit. They won't hit a topspin kicksmash over the fence or a drop shot because they aren't close to the net and because of the natural limitations of the backhand. Use your own shot to limit the possibilities of what can happen in the game.

2. **Predict based on movement:** How fast does your opponent react to your shot? Are they getting to the ball in time to be aggressive? What does their body position tell you? As soon as you watch your opponent move into position, you immediately know if they're able to hit certain shots. The list of possibilities immediately dwindles to a manageable level.

3. **Predict based on arm and racket:** The position of their arm and racket is a great final indicator of what shot they are going to hit. For example, let's say you've just hit a weak lob toward the middle of the court. The left-side player comes over and sets themselves up in the trophy position underneath the ball. You immediately think, okay, it's either going to be a full power smash or a fake smash down the centre. You position yourself in front of the line ready to sprint

---

6   Claude Shannon (1950). "Programming a Computer for Playing Chess" (PDF). Philosophical Magazine. 41 (314). Archived from the original (PDF) on 2020-05-23.

up the court, but you lock eyes on their arm and racket. As soon as you see them slow the takeback, you spot the fake smash for what it is and you react accordingly!

Predicting the game takes time and intentional practice. At first, it's enough to focus on your own strategies and techniques, but over time, as you progress, it's time to focus on the other team and reading the game as a whole.

Controlling Time and Space on the Court

When I started playing this complex sport I hardly thought about what I was doing. I brought over everything I knew about tennis and just did the best I could, listened to my coaches, and followed the lead of more experienced partners. This lack of thinking too hard helped propel me to my first tournament victory, but since then, I've realised that padel tactics involve a heavy measure of controlling court positioning and your team's readiness to defend. Navigating a match successfully is controlling, to the best of your ability, what happens on the court. You have more control than you might think.

Good technique means you can focus on controlling the speed of the ball.

Controlling time means hitting the ball faster or slower depending on what is happening in the match. Let's say, for example, your partner, who's playing on the right side, has been getting pummelled for the last five or six rallies. Your opponents have put you in the fridge (a tactic we'll dissect later) and are only playing on him. Your partner just returned yet another tough ball with a nice medium lob. The next shot finally goes to you, and you can tell your partner isn't quite set. What should you do? You could use this as an opportunity for a fast body shot to their right-side net player, but if you do, and they hit a fast block to your partner who's out of breath and not set, it might put them on the defensive yet again. A better shot would be a high lob to give your partner a chance to take a breath, reset, and continue the rally.

When you think about it, controlling time is why a fast smash can be a great shot. You're hitting a fast ball and not giving your opponent time to react. When you eventually learn how to do a kicksmash you will force your opponent out of the court if they want to have any hope of returning the ball. On the other side of the spectrum, learning how to play soft has time-controlling advantages as well. As you master playing softer, you give yourself time to come closer or farther from the net, depending on what your opponent decides to do. Mastering control of time opens up many new doors to win your matches. Get excited thinking about all the possibilities.

Controlling space is hitting into the spaces left open by your opponents. This is something you will learn to do from the very first time you step on the court. For beginners, it's just hitting the ball over the net. As you progress, it's keeping your eyes on the ball, but beginning to use your peripheral vision to see where your opponents are at any given moment. It could be hitting a ball that forces your opponents to move to reach it, hitting it down to their feet to force an awkward return, or playing safer balls into the middle to keep the rally going.

Combine these two elements of controlling time and space and you will become a force to be reckoned with on the court. Don't let the other team dictate the pace of the game. Take control and change the game into something that works for you.

The Chiquita: A Brilliantly Effective Soft Shot to the Feet

Hitting soft and down to the feet of the volleyer is called a chiquita in Spanish. It's the shot for changing the speed of the game, aggressively taking the net by surprise, or to use as a potential winner when you see your opponent drift into no man's land.

The technique for this shot is usually the same as the forehand and the backhand from the back of the court. Either after the glass or before, contact in front of your hip with flat contact. If you're learning this shot, or you're relatively new to the game, I recommend flat contact. If you're more advanced, practise hitting this shot with a little bit of slice, or even with a bit of topspin like the professionals might use and see how it feels for you.

A big part of using the chiquita effectively is understanding what is happening on the other side of the court. If you're able to track (and eventually predict) your opponent's movements, you'll begin to see how effective this shot can be. When you hit a short lob several times in a row, you'll sometimes notice your opponents drift back in anticipation of defending and keeping the net. When they do this, they leave a big gap in front of them which you can take advantage of. This might be a good time to block that ball down to their feet and make them either hit a half volley or force them to let it bounce first. This type of change in rhythm keeps them honest, likely giving you space behind them to hit a lob as they move forward to respond.

The chiquita is an excellent way to change the speed of the game, especially at the more advanced levels. For example, let's say you just hit a fast return to the body of the volleyer. Now is a good time to change the speed of the game by surprising them with a slower shot to their feet. Either way, you're moving the volleyer around and trying to open up space in the court in the front, the sides, or the back for a lob.

A shot you often see at the professional level is to hit down to the feet and then come in and volley the next one over the top to be able to keep the net. This is a risky play because if you don't put enough power into the shot you're exposed at net, but it's worth trying from time to time. Hitting side angles or another shot down to the feet is much less risky than trying to hit past their approaching partner or the partner who is in their net position. You might see whole points in the World Padel Tour where they're playing angles to the sides to force an opening before they get that chance to either lob or to hit through a gap. They'll often play a chiquita to respond to a chiquita. They don't do this to win the point, but to keep the status quo and keep the game going.

Common errors with the chiquita include:

- **Hitting too much topspin or slice:** As mentioned, it's perfectly fine to hit this shot with some spin, but you need not go crazy. Don't feel the need to put massive amounts of spin on the ball because you're more likely to make a mistake. Padel rackets don't have strings so you can't generate as much speed or spin as you could with a tennis racket. It's important to try to hit this shot soft and flat to let gravity do its thing and bring the ball down.

- **Hitting a chiquita when opponents are too close to the net:** There's no point in using this shot when your opponents are close because they have time to step in even closer to the net and finish the point. Hit the shot when they're at the second post or whenever you have enough space in front to aim for it. Hit softly into the gap and then either come forward on that ball or lob the next one to push them back and reclaim the net.

- **Not learning this shot or being too nervous to try it:** If you hit a really good chiquita you'll force your opponents to volley the ball up. This is a great opportunity to approach quickly and then either hit down on that next volley, putting them under pressure, or come in quickly and play a lob if you've got space behind them.

The chiquita is an effective weapon in the padel player's arsenal because it gives you options on the court. The more options you have, the more frustrating and difficult you will be to play against.

Capitalising on Your Strengths

I've always been good at moving forward into the net and volleying. This part of my game isn't necessarily a secret weapon, but it's where I am most comfortable. When I step onto the court, my partner knows I'm going to play fast and aggressively take the net position and he follows my lead. I'm not careless, but I confidently take the net using a variety of shots. Once I am at the net, my volleys are strong which makes it quite difficult for our opponents to regain their footing, especially if they weren't expecting me to be at net so quickly. With my years of tennis experience and naturally fast reaction speed, it's difficult to get a ball past me by force when I am in front.

The point is, I know my strengths quite well. Do you know yours?

You don't need to have a go-to weapon in padel to find success. Tennis players might have a killer serve or an unbelievable backhand, but in padel, most regular shots are returnable unless you are playing at a high level. Using your strengths doesn't mean hitting the ball as hard as you can. It means using finesse and your ability to read what is happening in the game to adjust on the fly.

When you're on the court and need to win, focus on your strengths. Use time away from competition to level up your weaknesses, but when you're playing to pull out the victory, use your best assets. Be confident in the skills and tactics you bring to the court. Don't be afraid to try new things to surprise your opponents, just make sure you have confidence in the shot. Capitalise on what works for you to win points.

Determine what you're best at and do more of this on the court. If you're best at the net and feel comfortable blocking balls, put yourself into the position to be able to do more of this. If you have a strong topspin smash, but don't yet have an aggressive vibora, confer with your partner and figure out a way to create more opportunities for you to use it. If you feel comfortable in the back, play a more defensive game and force your opponent to make mistakes. Put your best foot forward for each point.

Playing with your strengths is not only helpful on a skill level, but is good for the tactical element of the game. When I am coaching new students, I always impress upon them to focus on tactics whenever their game becomes challenging or they are losing. You might be missing shots for a technical reason, but have a discussion with your partner on what you can do tactically in the match to course correct. Consider what each of you is best at on the court, what your opponents find difficult, and make a tactical plan to overcome.

The Number-One Padel Tactic: Consistency

The pair that makes the most errors loses the match. Make the fewest errors while maintaining accuracy and confidence and you will win ninety-nine out of one hundred matches. You don't have to hit incredible smashes or cheeky drop shots to win the point. You're not playing in the World Padel Tour where they're forced to hit incredible (but risky!) winners because the point just won't end. If you keep the rally going long enough, you'll eventually force your opponent to make a mistake. Winning is as delightfully simple as this.

> *Most points at a club level are lost, not won. Focus on making less mistakes than your opponents rather than hitting more winners.* —Max Marsh Pickard, Dubai

This tactic is the reason you'll see teams who don't appear to be physically strong winning at lower-level tournaments. They know that consistency is king in this sport, and that younger, more inexperienced players will try to force the game to go a certain way. Consistency is more than just returning the ball over the net, it means being accurate with your shot placement and being able to repeat this accuracy. Consistent players who return the vast majority of balls will quickly find they rise to greater heights as their winning streak begins.

Here are five tips for training consistency:

1. **Don't rush the net:** Unless you're really good at safely taking the net, don't feel the need to rush forward super fast. Tennis players are notorious for chipping and charging which can work sometimes, but this shouldn't become a habit. The first objective of building the point is to take the net. Be patient, wait for the right ball, hit a lob or a nice chiquita, and then advance your position.

2. **Gain confidence from the back for each match:** From the start of the match, grow in your confidence to return the balls being sent your way. Notice any patterns from your opponents and get comfortable returning balls from this position. Gain confidence to thrive in the back as long as necessary.

3. **Take your time when at net:** Stay in control and play consistently into the corners or down the middle with multiple setup balls. You'll be surprised at how many points you'll finish because you played "safe" and created an opportunity for your opponents to make a mistake. Be patient and take your time. You're aiming to produce an easy ball you can finish with certainty. If you get lobbed

and have to start all over, no worries, this is guaranteed to happen. Retake the net and start your quest over again.

4. Conserve your energy throughout the match: If you're rushing around the court searching for the best position for every shot, you'll tire quickly. Then your opponents will notice you are running ragged and will press their advantage. Return to your starting positions whether in the front or back and play calmly to keep your energy level even.

5. Establish a repeatable technique for all of your shots: Practise good form and technique to vary your serve, ensure your bandeja to the middle bounces exactly where you want it to, and hit your volleys with just enough slice to keep your opponents on the defensive.

Hit each shot with accuracy and intention and your errors will decrease drastically. As a result, you'll grow in consistency and win more games.

Vary Your Game to be Unpredictable

Don't be the player who is always going for the kicksmash, counters the lob with a lob ten out of ten times, or plays every single shot to the same side. At a higher level, players will quickly adjust and it will become more difficult for you as the match goes on. Even if you try to play defensively by hitting quality bandejas you will quickly find your angles cut off if you play to the exact same spot every time.

The point with this tactic is to improve upon consistency and become consistently unpredictable. Notice what shots you tend to hit the most within specific situations and change your tactics. The fake smash, which we'll get to later, is a great way to change the speed of the game, but you need only consider varying based on what you've already done in the match. If you can't hit a kicksmash out of the court, your opponents won't be fooled by a fake smash. And further, if you start kicksmashing every ball out the side of the court, what's to stop them from running outside and being prepared every time you reel back to strike?

Consider what it would look like to change your game as you've played it so far in the match. What shots are your opponents already expecting?

Do you only ever hit it to the middle of the court? How could you change it up to throw your opponents for a loop? This tactic involves an ability to step away from the game to analyse how to improve. It's tough, especially if you're losing, but the better you and your partner get at righting the ship before it sinks, the quicker you will be able to recover. Figure out what the other team expects of you, then surprise them with something different.

You'll find that, beyond consistency, varying your game will be a tactic you'll need more and more often as your level increases. Your opponents will be much better at noticing any weaknesses early and capitalising on them. If you happen to win your first set most of the time, but you also tend to lose more and more points as the game goes on, this might mean your opponents caught on to your play styles and have now adjusted accordingly. Don't let them snatch the momentum away from you! Strike back by varying your shots.

The 70% Rule

You don't need to be able to hit a kicksmash out of the court, a drop shot that trickles out the side door, or an overly aggressive vibora deep into the corner to win points. All you have to do is be the last team to hit the ball over. In the end, racket sports are really this simple.

Always ask yourself before each shot you take: What is the percent chance I have of not missing? Am I comfortable with hitting this shot at a high percentage? If the answer is less than 70%, don't take the risk. So many players at this stage, guys especially, want to make the big winner to take home the game. But at this level, most points are lost due to unforced errors.

At the pro level, they need to make aggressive shots to finish the game. And even when they do, their opponents are so strong at defence that it often doesn't end the point. But if you're not playing at this level, your confidence in the shot needs to be high in order to make it worth the risk. It's far more likely that if you can keep the rally going long enough your opponents will make a mistake. Winning that way might not be as satisfying, but winning is winning, right?

At your next game, focus on improving your percentages of winners to unforced errors. You can keep track if you feel the need, but sometimes focusing on the improvement versus just playing to win will help you on your quest. At some point you will have to push it and make mistakes in order to improve. Pick your times appropriately. Master the 70% rule by being patient and only making the shots you are ready for when in competition mode.

• •

Get on the Court

Reflection: *What are your biggest strengths and most frustrating weaknesses?*

Action: *Speak to your partner about what they believe are your biggest strengths and weaknesses. Do their thoughts line up with yours?*

CHAPTER NINE
Don't Let the Plateau Stop You

Competing is a privilege. Make the most of the opportunity by pushing yourself to the limit of your abilities.

—Tony LaRussa

In 2019, there was no driving force behind creating the best possible English-speaking padel content accessible to everyone. The Padel School was born to meet this need. It's our mission to give each individual student exactly what they need to succeed and push through their barriers. What started as a few videos very quickly coalesced into a full-blown community replete with information on a variety of subjects. We also focus on coach education and filling the padelsphere with coaches who not only play at a high level and understand the game, but also possess the necessary ingredient of knowing how to get this information across to their students.

At The Padel School, we truly believe everyone should have access to the highest quality coaching.

You deserve to have the absolute best information right at your fingertips. This need for improving the game at a fundamental level all over the world drives me forward. The Padel School helps coaches help players avoid the dreaded plateau. The right information delivered in an effective way at the appropriate time helps you succeed. The game desperately needs more well-rounded coaches, better information, and easy access for players to get exactly what they need.

I hope to empower you to seek out the best information you can find and to spot bad advice before it leaves a permanent mark. The truth is, there are very few players at this stage who don't have some bad habits or style that could be improved. Maybe you're one of the lucky few who started out only having lessons and not playing with your friends ten times in between each lesson. More likely, you became obsessed and started playing several times per week.

The prerogative of this chapter is to get you where you want to go. If you've received poor advice, developed bad habits because you didn't know any better, or just can't seem to improve despite hours and hours of effort, there is likely something holding you back. Unfortunately for you, unless you live in an area with the best coaches in the world, you're going to have to figure this out yourself. I'm working with my team to expand as fast as possible, but for now, your advancement rests squarely on your shoulders and your ability to actualize the right information.

It's absolutely possible for you to improve and make progress. It might feel painful at first, but with time, something inside of you will click and you'll make incredible progress. Drew Brees, one of the best American Football quarterbacks of all time, had these thought-provoking words to say on progress:

You are either getting better or getting worse, but you are never staying the same.

I couldn't agree more. You are either getting worse or getting better, but there is no such thing as neutral momentum. When you come face-to-face with your first plateau it will either defeat you and drive you back or you will succeed.

Fight Through the Plateau

I had a bit of a different journey than most players. Since I was able to carry over my tennis acumen, I played at a high level almost straight away. I didn't go through a typical journey at a recreational level to get where I am now. I didn't experience the same challenges many players face, although I see plateaus playing out all the time with players I coach.

> *Whenever playing in competitions, if I felt my level had plateaued, I would always revert back to the basics. Often I've found that trying too much or over complicating the game, particularly in competition play, leads to errors and, ultimately, worse results. If I've done this, then I would go back to playing solid padel, structuring the points with correct patterns, and giving myself and partner the best opportunity to finish the points.* —Toby Bawden

My personal plateau came at a time when competition around me hit a wall while I was in Dubai. I wasn't able to find other players who could challenge me at a high enough level for me to compete internationally. I am far from one of the best players in the world, but I share this to say that your plateau will likely be unique depending on a variety of factors. You might be missing technique on a few skills, misunderstanding basic tactics, or you might not be at the level of fitness required to play for hours and hours in a weekend tournament. You might also just be like me and live somewhere where the competition isn't as fierce.

Eventually, I conquered my plateau by moving and changing locations, gaining a deeper tactical understanding of the game, and practising implementation. As padel becomes more and more popular, high-level competitions will take place around the globe, but I couldn't wait for this. My only choice was to find a new place to play.

It's common for players to hit a plateau. In fact, it's an almost unavoidable part of improving at any sport. There will come a time when no matter how hard you push, it will feel like a solid barrier has been dropped between where you are and where you want to go. It will feel impassable. I see it happen all the time. It dropped before me, and it will drop before you, too. However, you can minimise your time spent stuck there. If you're currently on a plateau and not seeing improvement, you can break free of its bonds.

The most common plateau players face is not having the correct advice based on their specific needs. There's a reason you aren't progressing, and it's likely something you're doing wrong either with your technique or on the court with your tactics. Here are some common complaints across a variety of levels:

- *I just can't seem to win any of my matches…*

- *My partner is improving quickly and I fear he's going to reach the next level and move on without me…*

- *I don't know how to hit a bandeja, so I just don't bother…*

- *I do really well in training but I can't seem to carry the skills over to a match…*

- *I can't seem to break the bad habits I know I have, no matter how hard I train…*

What is your plateau? How do you plan to overcome it?

The first step for breaking through the wall is to recognize what holds you back. This might take asking for feedback from your partner and/or your opponents (if they are willing to share), watching a recording of your matches to see how your opponents are beating you, or even finding a new coach who can give you a fresh perspective on your game as a whole. Once you discover what holds you back from your potential as a player, the final step is to keep going until you break through the wall. Keep playing matches even if you're losing, hit a bucket of balls every day for a week, or have a lesson dedicated to fixing your main issue. Keep going until you overcome it.

In the rest of this chapter we'll discuss several other strategies for breaking out of the plateau and advancing your level.

Stop Playing So Much

In any professional sport there is almost always an off-season. League owners would make more money if there were games year-round, but they choose to close the doors for a time to give the players a well-deserved break. Playing year-round would likely mean a drastic increase in injuries and would be unsustainable in the long run. It wouldn't be safe for the players, and the fans would also lose if players like Agustín Tapia and Bea González injured themselves because they overplayed.

Follow the same pattern as the pros and adjust how many times per week you take to the court. If you play too much, with the wrong technique, you are only setting yourself up for injuries later on down the line. Beyond the horrific story of tearing my ACL that I shared earlier in the book, I've had my fair share of injuries and setbacks including back spasms, plantar fasciitis, rotator cuff issues, ankle problems, and more. The amount of reasonable playtime is entirely up to you, but listen to your body, not just your need for more padel.

Believe it or not, you can't continue to improve at a high level just by playing six, seven, or eight times per week. You're only going to hurt yourself and make it harder and harder to keep playing. The human body can't take an infinite amount of wear and tear. Try to improve too quickly with multiple strategies and you will often end up disappointed in yourself by the end of the night. It's unhealthy to play to excess.

Have you ever heard of burnout from a job? The same can happen in sports.[7] I can honestly say I don't have any plans to return to tennis in any form, and this is likely because I got so close to it and played/coached far too much for too long. I became so burnt out that I walked away without ever wanting to go back. To this day, I don't miss tennis.

To stave off burnout of your body and mind, mix other sports or exercises into your routine. This way you can develop other muscle groups while giving padel-specific areas a much-needed break. Here are three to get you started:

Seek medical advice before beginning any of these sports/exercises and only do what you feel comfortable with.

1. **Resistance training:** Functional movements help correct imbalances and are important to keep your mobility strong. Resistance training helps with the range and mobility of your muscles which helps prevent injury.[8] Don't overdo it here either, because doing too much too soon presents its own set of risks, but resistance train once or twice a week and you might just be able to kicksmash your way to victory.

2. **Swimming:** This is one of the best full-body exercises that improves cardio and doesn't restrict mobility. (Tip: do not swim on the day of padel or at least not before—the full-body action exhausts smaller muscle groups and usually leads to poorer technical skill execution.) Other forms of cardio, like running or cycling, are also beneficial to build stamina.

---

7   "When More Isn't Better: Dealing With Burnout in Competitive Sports – Women's Sports Foundation." Women's Sports Foundation, 15 Sept. 2016, www.womenssportsfoundation.org/inspiration/when-more-isnt-better-dealing-with-burnout-in-competitive-sports.

8   Fleck, S J, and J E Falkel. "Value of resistance training for the reduction of sports injuries." Sports Medicine (Auckland, N.Z.) vol. 3,1 (1986): 61-8. doi:10.2165/00007256-198603010-00006

3. **Pilates/yoga/mobility exercises:** One of the areas most players struggle with on court (often without realising it) is mobility. Working to improve this will likely help prevent injury.

4. **Play mind games:** Padel is one of the toughest mental games out there so it helps to have off-court training that lets sore muscles rest. Play chess, choose from a myriad of online strategy games, or play a game like Scrabble with your family (especially if you are bad at it!). Work your mind to think more strategically so that you can strongly react to tough games.

There are many potential problems that could stymie your bid to keep playing padel, so watch out for this kind of physical and mental burnout. At this stage, you are enjoying the game and want to be able to keep playing. Be sensible about how many times per week you're playing to avoid injury and burnout. Add in other activities as appropriate. Even if padel is the activity that gives you the most joy, you don't need to play it every day.

Play Both Sides

I am more than happy to play on the left because I can be aggressive and attack. I feel less restricted and more free to send the ball whenever I want to change up the game and keep my opponents on their toes. But playing on the right is also fun because it's my responsibility to control the game. I am extremely analytical by nature, so I love watching and dissecting the other team in an effort to create opportunities for us to finish the point. My analysis of the game as a whole would be incomplete if I didn't have knowledge and experience with each side.

At this stage in your padel journey, you're likely settling on a side. Yet it's important to continue playing on the opposite side from time to time to expose yourself to what your partner will face on a regular basis. In fact, switching sides for a few matches is one of the best ways to overcome a plateau, as it forces you to mix things up and play differently. Playing on the side you aren't used to will open up your understanding and ability to read what your opponents are doing and will give you the tools you need to be able to adjust to various strategies.

> *Coming from a tennis background with a game style based around my serve, the ability to play the fast smashes from the beginning of my Padel career catered me to the left side. It was very easy for me to hit the 3m and bring the ball back—I feel this would be the same for most tennis players on the taller side with a good serve.* —Ross Taylor, Gold Coast, Australia

Typically, the characteristics of a left-side player differ from those of a right in subtle and not-so-subtle ways. The only exception is left-handed players must always play on the right. Unless you have a rare case where you're a left-hander playing with another left-hander (which doesn't happen very often), you'll want to be on the right to open up the middle to your forehand.

From the pros, left-side players include Agustín Tapia, Franco Stupaczuk, Alejandro Galán, Ariana Sánchez, and Bea González. Here are the basic characteristics of a left-side player:

- **Slightly more aggressive temperament:** The job of the left-side player is to finish points. This means you are going to be more aggressive when at the net when a nice juicy opportunity presents itself. You are patient in the back, but your goal is to take advantage of the setup volleys played by your partner.

- **Physically fit:** Left-side players tend to be faster and physically fitter due to the demands of the game from that side. They quickly move up and down the court to the net to block or attack and then return to the back to play defence. Left-side players generally have the endurance necessary to keep going as long as needed to finish the match. This higher level of aggression takes a toll on your energy over time and the longer your stamina lasts at this high level, the more games you will win.

- **High overhead confidence/ability:** To be most effective on the left, you'll need to have a high comfort level with most of the overheads available to you. Typically, the player on the left side will come to the middle and take most of those balls with their forehand. Depending on the depth of the ball that comes your way, you'll want to be comfortable hitting an aggressive vibora or a topspin smash.

From the pros, right-side players include Alejandra Salazar, Federico Chingotto, and Martín Di Nenno. Here are a few characteristics of a right-side player:

- **Cool, calm, and collected:** Have you ever played against someone on the right who hits everything back? And no matter what you sent their way, they remain unflappable? A great right-side player maintains the calmness required to win tight games. They keep control of the game and set up the ball for their more aggressive partner to finish.

- **The strategist of the pair:** It's this player's job to set up an easy ball for their partner to attack and finish the point. They can definitely be aggressive and finish points as the need arises, but over the course of a game the left-side player will finish the vast majority of the points. You'll see in many of the top teams in the World Padel Tour that the right-side player sets up and the left side finishes. Notable exceptions include Juan Lebrón who is an aggressive right-side player, and any left-handed player like Arturo Coello who plays on the right.

- **Consistent with defensive overheads:** Right-side players must be comfortable using the bandeja and, in particular, the higher bandeja for balls that are high up over your right shoulder. You'll also find that mastering the gancho, a shot we discussed previously, will help you keep the net and keep your opponents back. You'll find that you don't use the attacking vibora too often due to the need to move and get your feet around the ball.

- **Strong Smash:** The future of the game might be for every right-side player to have a strong smash like Juan Lebrón's, but only time will tell.

When it comes to choosing a side, it comes down to who you're playing with. Know their strengths, weaknesses, fitness levels, etc. As much as I don't like to admit it, I'm getting on a bit now, so it's taking me longer and longer to remain in peak physical condition at a point where I can be competitive. I need to be in excellent physical condition to play on the left. On the right side I can get away with a bit less conditioning because it's less intense physically and more about endurance.

Regardless of the side you choose, make sure you understand your role within the match. Decide with your partner how you are going to approach each point and complement each other. None of the above characteristics are written in stone, so don't feel it's wrong if you are a fast aggressive player on the right. Communicate your intentions with your partner and work together to find the best approach that works for both of you.

Speed Date to Discover Your Padel Soul Mate

Ideally, when you're first playing the game, you'll be in a position where you're able to try a bunch of different partners so you can see what works and what doesn't. Think of finding a partner as akin to speed dating in real life. Set up several matches with different players and switch partners as you go. Calculate what you like about certain players and what works best to complement your game. Playing with different partners exposes you to various playstyles, and can help you overcome certain plateaus, especially if you are open to feedback.

Remember, you don't have to pick just one person forever. It's perfectly okay to play with a variety of partners. Even players at the World Padel Tour level have been known to switch things up after a few years. This even includes players at the top like Juan Lebrón, a previous left-side player in peak physical condition, proving to be very effective on the right side with Alejandro Galán on the left. Eventually, it's better for progress' sake to enhance your current game with the same person, but you don't need to rush to find this.

An enjoyable exhibition game with Ale Galán in Dubai.

I know it isn't always possible to play with a variety of players. Maybe you're from a small town with only a handful of people who even know what this sport is. Maybe you've already risen to the top level in a city where padel is relatively new and the pool of players is extremely small. In this case, you might not be able to switch as often as you'd like for logistical reasons. Still, have hope that there are players out there who fit your playstyle perfectly. You just need to find them by playing often and meeting as many new players as possible. There is almost always someone else looking to mix things up and play with someone new.

Here is a checklist to use when searching for the perfect teammate. These aren't hard-and-fast rules, but use them to whittle down the playing field appropriately:

- ☐ **I like this person off the court:** Is the idea of hanging out with your current partner unbearable? The first step that many players miss is whether or not you would even like hanging out with this person if not for padel. You don't need to be best friends, but if you find yourself paired with someone you don't even like, it might be time to part ways. Never let the potential of a few wins here and there be the reason you play with someone who doesn't match your vibe.

- ☐ **I'm free to grow and experiment:** One of the best feelings a great partner will give you is freedom to learn and grow with the game. If you miss a smash because you're trying out a new topspin technique, they will support your endeavour to improve. Sure, you both could stay at your current level and be okay, but if your goal is to beat better teams, this level of freedom is a must. Players on the left side especially need support from right-side players so they can finish points with strong attacks that might be risky to pull off at first as they're learning.

- ☐ **This person fits my preferred temperament style:** I say "preferred" here because your partner need not be exactly like you. In fact, teams consisting of two unique personalities and play styles may even help to balance each other. Ask yourself: do I need someone level-headed who will bring calm to my side of the court, or do I need someone who will make sure we are both pumped up for the win? Sure, you'd love to play with someone who is going to help you win, but weigh the costs. Consider the long-term effects of picking the wrong partner, even if you do happen to be winning.

- ☐ **They elevate my game:** This is a tough item to measure initially. It can be as simple as tracking how many games you win with this person and how much trouble you give the other team, but it's often more nuanced. Likely, this comes down to the feeling you have during the game. Is your partner setting up the environment of the game for you to play your best? Do they have your back if you dash in to defend a drop shot, return it too short, and your opponent hits it behind you? A great team covers the entire court.

- ☐ **Their level is close to mine:** It's great to play against and with people who are better than you, but when your partner is significantly higher or lower in skill it can make things tricky. For one thing, it might become easier to place blame for losses thus creating tension. For another, the weaker partner is more easily targeted by the other team and this can lead to a mismatch or the stronger partner only playing a few points from time to time.

Don't be afraid to "leave" your partner if things aren't working out. Unless you signed a blood contract, there is nothing that says you can't play with someone else. Sure, feelings might get hurt along the way, but it isn't worth it in the short or long term to play with someone who is no longer a great fit.

Test Yourself in a Tournament or a League

At this stage, you're starting to think about what it might be like to join a more serious tournament or league. I say, go for it! You can play with the same group of friends all you want, but it's not going to test your level. One of the best ways you can quickly improve and blast through plateaus is to join a local tournament and/or a league. A tournament is a great way to test your skills and overall prowess at the sport, and a league will give you more opportunities for regular matches against opponents at your level. Battling other teams who are also journeying towards improvement is a surefire way to establish yourself as a strong contender.

Many of my students find themselves in increasing levels of competition and not all of them feel the same about it. Some find it fun, while others prefer to just play with friends, and this is perfectly okay. However, if you decide to pit yourself against other teams in heavier competition, here is what I suggest you do to maximise your takeaways:

- **Take it semi-seriously:** Go into the game wanting to win. If you're competitive like me, you won't have this problem. But don't take it too seriously either. You can't control the outcome. With four players on the court who all want to win, there's way too much going on for you to be in full control. All you can do is to control your response to the game. Keep a level head throughout and find just the right balance between competition and fun.
- **Always communicate with your partner:** Keep your partner aware of how you are doing throughout the competition. Make sure you both stay on the same page. One of the best things you can do is

to talk before the game about how you want to handle losses or setbacks. Ask them how you can best support them if they start to go off track, and give them useful tips for dealing with you as well.

- **Make improvement the goal:** As long as you come away learning something about yourself, your team, or the game as a whole, you're a winner. Sure, winning the actual tournament or league would be satisfying, but only one team gets to claim victory. Are all the other teams who signed up losers? Yes, but only if they don't take something away from the loss. If all you do is go home sad and pissed off because you lost, you'll likely lose the next tournament, too.

Stop playing so much padel that your arm feels dead at the end of the week. Find the best partner for you and don't settle for less. Test your mettle in a tournament or league and push yourself to the brink. Make a note of your current strengths and weaknesses on the court. (Yes, physically write it down with pen and paper.) Continue to improve your game by going to the court again and again. Blast through the inevitable plateau by sheer force.

Get on the Court

Reflection: What plateau are you facing right now that impedes progress?

Action: After your next game, take written notes of your struggle areas and bring this to your coach or training partner. Discuss what holds you back and work hard to improve.

CHAPTER TEN
Begin Your Domination

Firstly, you want to love what you're doing, if you're not loving what you're doing don't do it. You have to be passionate about it. If you want to be the best, you have to learn, watch the games and players, watch the person in your position or doing what you want to do.

—David Campese, Wallabies legend

The further you go in padel, the more complex the tactics and shots become. And of course, the more difficult the shot, the more time and energy it will take to get it right. As you dig in and master each skill, try not to rush the process. Let the skill flow as naturally as possible to eventually use it on command without thinking too hard.

Returning the Serve Near 100%

When I started my padel journey I missed many returns from serves into the glass. I would always try to take them early, before the glass, and block them over the net. This sometimes worked, but as serves came faster and faster, it stopped working. I had to become friends with the glass. Eventually, as long as I was in the right position with my racket back and prepared, I found that I could return nearly 100% of serves. Backhand slice serves, left-handed anomalies, and the occasional fast topspin serve didn't scare me. I returned them all. You will too.

The padel serve is used to start the point, it's not an offensive weapon. It eventually becomes necessary to return the serve at near 100%. At the World Padel Tour level, it's rare for anyone to miss a serve return. When they do miss, it's not because the serve was amazing or impossible to defend, it's likely just a misstep or a misread on their part. Watch any player at this level miss a serve return and you will see disappointment etched upon their face.

As your level rises, you'll notice infrequent occasions when an ace finishes a point. This high level of success expected from the serve returner is really weird to get used to because there's no wiggle room. It's nerve racking to know you should have responded to a tough serve but missed for whatever reason. Coming from tennis, I was used to serving aces and being aced myself on occasion, but that's just not how padel works.

But what shot do you hit for the serve return? Here's how I simplify it for students:

- **The serve bounces fast into the glass:** Hit a block or a chiquita back to the server.

- **The serve lands near the middle T:** Hit a lob off this shot. Your opponent is hoping to get you out of position, so don't take the bait. If you hit a short and fast ball, it might give them time to hit into your corner, putting you into a difficult position. The lob is best, especially if you have to stretch to reach the ball as it gives you time to recover your position.

- **The serve is a slower second serve or goes to the middle:** Don't be afraid to be aggressive here. Hit a deep lob, a short chiquita, or a fast shot to the body.

Eventually, you'll move past these recommendations and create your own style and flair. The last thing you want is to be too predictable, so ensure you vary your serve returns to keep your opponents on their toes.

Defending the Glass: Back, Side, and Double Glass

Improving confidence with the glass helps you build the points from the back of the court.

There are so many different ways the ball can bounce off the glass on the court. It's one of the most difficult aspects of the game but also the most fun when you finally improve. We covered the glass a bit earlier, but now I want to share the next step, which is moving beyond just using the glass to get the ball back to defending strongly so you can keep the point alive and keep things from getting desperate. We'll cover each of the many possibilities of how the ball can bounce, and what you can do to tie up any loose ends in your defensive game.

Back Glass

Judge the contact point and figure out where you need to move in order to put yourself into the best position possible when the ball bounces off the back glass. The best kept secret is to take the racket back in early preparation at the height of where you are eventually going to hit the ball. So many players bring the racket up far too high for lower balls and then end up swatting at the ball at the last minute. This wild swing can work sometimes, but often leads to an error. Get behind the ball and hit through it with control.

If you struggle to know which balls to attack and which balls to defend off the back glass, think about a traffic light:

- **Green:** It's a high bounce so feel free to attack the ball. Don't forget that it's more than acceptable to attack from the back of the court if you have the opportunity to do so.
- **Yellow:** If the ball is about waist height, hit a neutral shot like a chiquita or maybe even a lob.
- **Red:** For low balls stay defensive. You don't have the angle required to do anything fancy with the ball. Most importantly, get behind the ball and get low to pick it up.

Side Glass

Mastering the side glass is another tricky part of improving your court awareness and flexibility. You'll see this type of shot most often on the serve so this will be an especially helpful area to work on as you aim to return the serve at 100%.

Do you remember the ready, read, react we shared earlier in the book? Use that here for any shot off the glass. Get back into ready position as quickly as possible after the last shot. Read what the incoming back is going to do. React by moving into the correct location as soon as you can accurately predict the ball's movement.

When practising the side glass, think back to our lesson from chapter eight on creating time and space. Give yourself plenty of time to react to any ball with the space to take the shot. Sometimes the ball is going to "stick" to the side (meaning it doesn't come far enough away from the glass) and become very difficult to return. In this case, all you can do is get the racket ready for your best guess as to where the ball is going to be and then block accordingly. Other times, you'll want to let the ball bounce off the side glass and come to you.

For example, think about what it looks like when you have a server hitting with a bit of topspin and standing to the far side. With the angle of the topspin ball coming into the glass, it's going to bounce off quite far. You could take this before the glass, but it's far easier (and better) to let it bounce and come off. This will give you plenty of time and space to hit a calculated return.

Prepare early by pulling your racket back before the ball even bounces off the side glass. Move your feet into position and get behind the ball, following through with a short and compact swing.

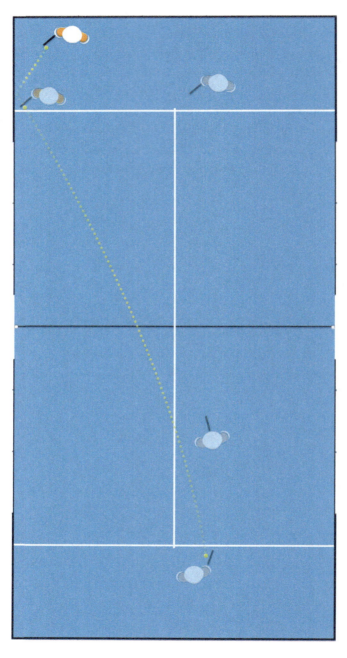

Image 10: Defending the side glass.

Double Glass

Defending against the double glass can be a player's worst nightmare, but like all nightmares, someday you'll wake up and no longer be afraid. Sure, you've gotten used to the side and back returns, but now you have to put them together. It's not uncommon for a player to advance their level quite high, yet still be unable to defend against the double glass when put under moderate pressure.

Like any glass shot it takes getting used to. It's important to stop trying to block every ball that comes your way, and just let it do its thing, even if it means it's going to be difficult at first. Always remember that the glass buys you time to respond. Even if the shot comes in at a high velocity, you will always have a bit more time to respond if you let it bounce and hit the glass.

One drill we often do with our players is to have them shout "side!" or "back!" when learning how to respond to the double glass. Reading where the ball is going to hit first will be your marking point for where the ball is going to end up after bouncing off the second glass (side or back). The sooner you can tell which glass the ball is going to strike first, the sooner you can get yourself into the right position to respond.

When a ball comes from the cross court at medium speed and hits deep on the side glass first, don't panic! Move your feet accordingly, taking quick little steps to get into position, prepare your racket, and then hit the ball. If the ball comes at a high speed off the back glass and rebounds into the side glass, move toward the glass and prepare. Use the same traffic light system we mentioned early to know when to attack or defend. Don't sweat it if this is difficult at first. Keep practising.

As always, make sure you are behind the ball, take your racket back, and hit the ball out in front of you. Give yourself more space so that even if you do have to lunge after the ball, you'll have enough room to do so.

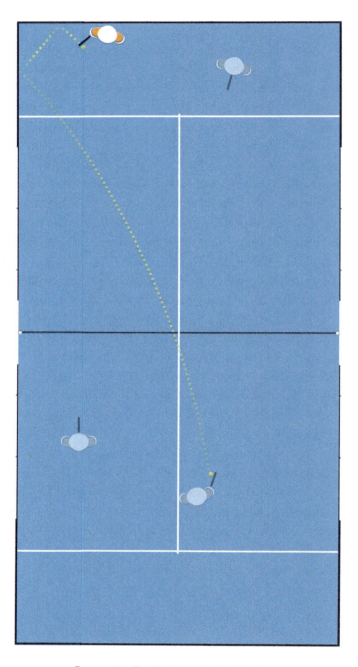

Image 11: Defending the double glass.

Back/Side Glass Boast

Using the back or side glass should always be a shot of last resort. If you have time to get around the ball to hit a clean shot, it's much better to do this than using a boast. If you have time and space, don't use the back or side glass to get the ball over. Not using the glass ensures much more control and less risk. The only times you want to use the back or side glass boast is when you are trying to be tricky, or when you are desperate to hit the ball over one more time.

Sometimes, throughout the course of a point, the ball will get behind you, and you'll have no choice but to use the glass to return. 99% of the time your shot choice from this defensive position is the lob when using the back glass. The closer you are to the glass, the better, as it will allow you to hit the right angle for a lob, but of course this is not always within your control. It's much better to play defensively to regain the momentum of the point. Play a lob, return to ready position, and rebuild the point from there.

For the side glass, it's typical to use this as a last resort if you're out of position. Most of the time, a ball played off the side glass could have just as easily been hit normally. Still, it can be an effective shot to add a bit of spin to the ball. It's also an incredible amount of fun to try to work it into a game, and it can be extremely satisfying to win a point this way. A word of caution though: Don't overuse the side glass as a boast. It's difficult to get right, and it's next to impossible to hit a lob with it. You might be able to hit an effective chiquita, but more often than not, the ball is going to float over the net and a strong opponent will make you pay. Use it to mix up the game and vary your shots from time to time, but don't rely on it too much.

Attacking with the Volley

Once you become more comfortable with the volley as a shot, you'll get better and better at using it to finish points. When thinking about winning the point off a volley, a three-step approach helps to break things down, regardless of how exactly you end up hitting a winner.

1. **Take the net:** 99% of the time you can't hit a winning volley from the back or middle of the court. Take the steps necessary to take the net and then progress towards hitting a winner.

2. **Hit one to three setup volleys as needed:** If your opponents are in a good position, it's very difficult to hit a winning volley. Even if you get a really easy ball, it's not easy to finish the point because they're in a good position to cut off the angles and block the ball right back to you. A good setup volley forces your opponents into a difficult position which gives you space to hit a killer volley. Move your opponent around with as many setup volleys as needed until they are out of position and struggling to return the ball.

3. **Finish the point:** Win the point by hitting into the spaces and forcing a difficult ball for your opponents. Recognize your opponent's body position and their placement on the court. If they are far back, hit a short drop shot. If they are slightly leaning to one side or the other, use power to send the ball out of their reach to one side. If they are drifting into no man's land, hit a strong shot at their feet.

Most points are won at the net, so volleys should be a key focus of your training.

Taking the net is the first step, hitting several setup volleys to build the point is the next, and then taking advantage of open space is the final part of the process. Approach each shot with the intention of ramping up to a potential winner.

Using an Attacking Bajada off the Back Glass

True or false: *When a ball bounces off the back glass, your only option is to defend.*

False. You got it right! If your opponent hits a deep lob that bounces high off the back glass, you can (and should!) attack the ball and make it difficult for your opponents. This doesn't mean you can't hit a lob or a chiquita from this position, but the bajada is a great shot if you want to regain control of the point.

For the attacking bajada, you need to pick the right ball. If the ball bounces too low off the back glass, "sticks" to the back glass, or hits the top fence and spins away randomly, your options become limited. But if the ball comes far enough away from the glass, and you're in a good position, hit the ball with speed and spin.

The trick to hitting this shot properly is to quickly move back into position to get behind the ball on your forehand side if possible. Sometimes you won't be able to get into position fast enough to be on your forehand side, which is okay, but default to this position whenever possible. The error I see most often with players who struggle with the bajada is not moving back fast enough. For whatever reason, they see the lob come over their heads and don't move fast enough to get into position. Your options become limited if you move slowly and take your time, but if you move quickly you can make a decision based on where the ball is going to bounce.

Hit through the ball with moderate speed either down the middle or to your open side cross court. As you begin to feel more comfortable, increase your racket speed and hit it harder, but remember that a nice and slow controlled shot with spin works wonders too. When considering where to aim the ball, play it safe and stick to the middle or cross court, as hitting down the line is more risky. Each time you hit it during the match, switch things up to always keep your opponents guessing.

If all else fails when you're trying to attack off the back glass, remember the lob is perfectly fine. This is especially true if your opponents are expecting you to attack strongly and are sticking to the net like white on rice. If they're up close and your teammate calls this out to you, why not hit a fast lob to regain the net position? Mix it up and don't just default to the "right" shot or what is expected. Continue to practise unpredictability and shot variance.

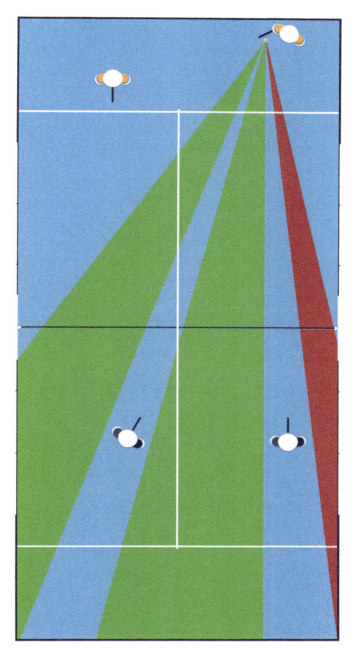

Image 12: Bajada aiming direction.

Upgrade Your Topspin Smash to the Fence

As we continue our discussion on the value of unpredictability, the topspin smash to the fence is one of the best smashes to use. Think about what happens when the ball hits the glass: It's predictable and will do roughly the same thing every time. But what happens when the ball hits the fence? No one knows where it's going. Introducing randomness into the game is a great strategy and another way to increase your variability and, ultimately, your win percentage.

The trick with this shot is choosing the right ball to hit. Generally, the topspin smash is used for a ball hit over your left shoulder that you don't have time to come under for a full-power smash, or to the side to hit an aggressive vibora. When you see the right ball, move your body under it in the topspin trophy position, hit with medium to high speed above the normal eye height of the Bandeja (to reduce the risk) and aim for a spot on the court to the diagonal just before the fence. Hitting too slow will give your opposition time to move forward and block, and if you hit too fast, your risk of making a mistake increases, and the ball will bounce higher making it easier to defend.

Proper form for trophy position.

It will take time and match practice to work out when this shot is best for your game. As you're learning, practise hitting with varying speeds and spin until you find the right combination. Take a bucket of balls and a partner and have them hit balls of varying heights over your left shoulder. Practise getting into position as quickly as you can, brushing up the ball with topspin, and then aiming at different spots in front of the fence to feel out what works.

Practising the topspin smash to the fence is an excellent precursor to mastering the kicksmash, which we will discuss later. It helps you get comfortable with the unique positions required, like loading from the legs, arching the back, and brushing up the back of the ball. Master this topspin smash down to the fence, and you'll be hitting the three-metre smash in no time.

Yes, Hit Hard with the Flat Smash

You'll normally hear me, and just about every other coach in the padelverse, talk about the importance of slowing the ball down. On most of the shots in this game, it pays to play slow. But every once in a while, hitting hard and flat can throw the other team off balance. The best time to use this shot is when your opponents are defending near the back glass. Aim to hit the ball towards the player that is farther back or down the centre if both players are back.

The technique for hitting the shot is to set up in your normal bandeja position with your feet facing the fence and your arms up. Let the ball drop to about eye height and then prepare your swing. Unlike the bandeja where you come down the ball a bit and slow the racket head speed, you'll pronate your wrist slightly into the contact point of the ball and then follow through. There should be zero spin on the ball, and a nice and flat trajectory. Aim to hit the ball down the line so it comes straight off the back glass giving your opponents less time or, if you can, hit the fence, or near the fence, for a confusing bounce.

Use this smash when your opponents are in the back of the court and you have enough time to set up and prepare for the shot. It's best used after you've already hit a few bandejas and your opponents are predicting what you are going to do. Don't overuse this shot because good players will be able to respond appropriately and even put you back under pressure.

When the right moment strikes, hit the ball with force to win the point.

Fool Me Once… Sneak Attack with a Fake Smash

Time slows down all around you. You can taste the sweat trickling down your face from your forehead. The ball is up and it's nice and juicy. As you gather all the energy left in your body, bend your legs, point your non-racket hand to the ball, and arch your back, you see something out of the corner of your vision. The enemy is taking the bait! Both players are sprinting to the net. One of them already has a foot out the side door. You hope your smile doesn't betray your intentions as you contact the ball, sending it slowly down the middle of the court with no chance for the other team to retrieve it. Other than a perfectly timed dropshot that goes out the side door, there's not a more satisfying way to win the point.

The fake smash is all about misdirection and reading the game. This takes comfort and familiarity with the variety of smashes. If you haven't already demonstrated an ability to hit a powerful smash, you won't fool anyone. This shot needs to come later in the match, after you've already won points from your smash. But if you do have a big smash, the fake smash is the next level of trickery to elevate your game to the next level.

The key to this smash is to be extremely selective, disguise your intentions by using the same form you would use on a regular smash, and then wait until the very last moment to switch to a slower racket speed. The best place to aim depends on where your opponents choose to move, but the middle is likely your best and safest option. All you are trying to do is get it past them so it bounces low at the other end. It doesn't even have to be a shot that ends the point as long as it stays low and forces them to hit another difficult ball which you can then pop out of the court.

Choose the exact right time to be sneaky and you will not only win points on your fake smash, you will probably catch your opponents off guard when they don't prepare for your full smash, giving you free reign to hit it as hard as you want. Do this and the enemy will fall right into your trap!

Get on the Court

Reflection: *Is my defensive game as good or better than my attacking game? What do I need to do to improve the weaker of these areas?*

Action: *Go with a partner and practise some of the more difficult shots—double glass, topspin smashes, fake smashes, etc., most of which can only be practised with a partner. This is a great chance for both of you to video the shots and pop them in our community!*

Stage Three
High-Level Competition

Chapter Eleven
Elevate

You are never too old to set another goal or to dream a new dream.

—C.S. Lewis

Trailing in the third set of the final match of a regional tournament in Madrid, my partner and I walked off the court for a changeover. The score was 6-5 and we were feeling the heat. I sat down, wiped the sweat from my forehead, and looked at my partner. He nodded and I nodded back. Wordlessly, we took to the court. We knew what we had to do and we would donate every last drop of sweat to the cause.

All eyes were on us. This was it. Our chance for victory hung on our ability to stay on serve. A tangible energy buzzed in the air. The crowd was tense but electric. I hoped we could make them proud. Nothing else mattered in that moment, only the next point. Our focus was locked in. My partner stepped up to the service line, I took my position at the net, and we were off.

We took the first point when our opponent on the left tried to be too aggressive and plunked the ball into the net. 15-0…

On the next point, my partner hit a four-metre off a weak volley to put us up 30-0…

Then, inexplicably, I missed an easy bandeja and put the ball into the fence instead. 30-15…

The next point became the highlight of the match. Both teams were on fire and no one wanted to admit defeat. On a simple bandeja on or around the 40th rally, our opponents struck the very tip of the net cord. I watched breathlessly as the ball hung in mid-air for a moment, and then dropped without a sound to the court below, far out of reach. 30-30…

A kicksmash from my partner put up 40-30 as our opponents read it incorrectly and didn't move out of the court in time to return…

Several rallies into the next point my partner hit the back glass because of an unlucky gust of wind (at least that's what he maintains to this day!). The score was 40-40…

This was it. If we won the golden point we'd force a tiebreak. If not, the victory would belong to our opponents. My partner served to the left-side player and it was on. After I popped up a ball that was too short, their right-side player hit a powerful vibora into my corner. I was slightly out of position from the last ball so I responded defensively and just barely got my racket on it, but I knew trouble as soon as I hit it… My lob was too short… They seized the opportunity and hit an easy four-metre to end our life in the tournament.

As soon as the game was over a mix of emotions flashed through my body. *Frustrated* I wouldn't be able to bring home the win for the team. *Mad* that I made the last error. *Appreciative* that I get to play this game that I love so much. Swirling emotions aside, I stood up, shook myself off, and walked to the net to congratulate the other team with a smile and a handshake.

Lose Well

Sometimes you win, sometimes you lose. It's impossible to not be disappointed when you make it so far into a game only to have the win snatched away from you, but it's important to exercise good sportsmanship even at the moment of a close defeat. I've won some major tournaments in tennis and in padel. I've also lost on many more occasions. Unless you're a superhero, the journey will be the same for you.

> *The only way to prove that you're a good sport is to lose.*
> —Ernie Banks

In any given tournament, most players will lose. It's important not to let losses get you down, and equally important to support your partner no matter what. Never play the blame game. You win and you lose together. There have been times the loss was all my fault, and times when my partner messed up. But no matter what, I accepted each loss with a friendly handshake and by saying, "Good luck in the tournament!"

I love competition. My parents and coaches nurtured this love in me at an early age. I'm driven to get as good as I can so that I play at my absolute best when it comes time for a match. I hope to encourage the same values in my daughter. I want her to love competition, but I never want her to feel the raging pressure to win that so many young athletes face.

Because I know what I'm playing for, I rarely get upset at myself or at my partner during or after a game. I take losses in stride and celebrate wins within the spirit of friendly competition. I've always wanted to win and to prove that I can play at my best, but good sportsmanship trumps my own feelings at any given moment, and it's a value I hope to impart to you throughout this chapter. As you play matches and improve, never forget you are playing against other people with similar goals; nobody jumps on the court hoping to lose!

Learning to lose well is the least "fun" strategy I will share in this book, but it's probably the most impactful. Go out and play at higher levels. Do everything in your power to win, but when the cards don't come up in your favour, keep your head up and soldier on. Take the losses in stride and celebrate your wins with aplomb.

Elevate Your Partnership

When you're at this stage of your padel journey, you likely have a consistent partner picked out. It doesn't mean you don't also play with other people from time to time, but when it comes to reaching a higher competitive level, you want a partner who brings out the best in you, and you in them.

What people don't know is that it's essential to ask yourself how *you* can be a better partner when on the court. It's much easier to place blame upon someone else when you start to lose, and harder to admit it's partly your fault even if your partner just hit seventeen unforced errors in a row. The best mantra for any team to have is that they win together and lose together. But the deeper truth is that you need to mean it. Don't use this as a cliché and then secretly blame your partner if they start falling behind or if they are the reason you keep losing. Revel in your wins and fight another day when you lose.

With my history of competitions as a player, coach, and commentator, I've seen several things that successful teams do well. Here's how you can be a better team:

- **Know strengths and weaknesses:** Figure out your strengths and weaknesses and discuss them with each other. The longer you play with the same person, the more you will discover each of you have things you're great at, and things that don't come as easily. This is not the time to be shy or afraid of feedback. The more open you can be as a team, the better off you will be in the long run.

- **Don't surprise your partner:** Balance your unpredictability against your opponents with a certain amount of predictability for your partner. This means not overly rushing the net, avoiding no man's land, or having a clear shot intention. Don't be so wild on the court that your partner never knows what you're going to do next.

- **Communicate effectively:** Strong communication is vital to any relationship, and the same goes for when you're on the padel court. It's important to go into each game with a concrete strategy. Talk to your partner for fifteen to thirty minutes before the match starts to catch up and get on the same page. If your partner has had a crap day and isn't mentally ready for the game, it's important for you to know this so you can adapt to their mood. And then, as the game progresses, continue speaking and changing your game plan as appropriate. Each time you change ends or there is a break in points, check in with your partner and redirect strategy as needed.

- **Talk on court:** Beyond the change of ends or breaks from the game, get used to talking while on the court. When your partner goes back to hit a bajada, tell them where your opponents are. Likely, they will be up front to block, but if not, letting your partner know can be very helpful for them to determine what shot they should hit. Be clear, concise, and call, "Mine!" or "Yours!" as early as possible.

- **Be positive.** It's incredibly important to be positive on the court, especially when your partner is struggling. If they are missing shots and you keep letting out audible sighs or grunts of frustration, it won't make them play any better. In fact, it'll probably only make things worse. Positive encouragement goes a long way toward developing a great partnership not only on the court. It helps foster a friendship that extends beyond the glass box.

Be the best partner you can be, and don't fret if things aren't working out right now. This isn't a relationship book by any means, but the perfect padel partner is out there somewhere. I said it before but I'll say it again: Don't feel stuck if your partner doesn't match the items on the checklist I mentioned in chapter nine, or you just don't feel like playing with them anymore. Move on if it's not a great fit. You and your current partner might just be better off without each other.

Play the Game of Whys after Your Match

> *It's not about being the best. It's about being better than you were yesterday.* —Florent Manaudou, Olympic gold medallist

The first step is to identify the problem you want to solve. It might be your technique for the bandeja, your inability to take the net, or the fact that you keep coming in second in your weekly competitions. Then ask yourself *why* as many times as needed in order to determine the root cause of the problem. This process isn't fun, but it can provide glimpses into why you lost or didn't play as well as you might have liked. You can come up with a plan to fix the problem only if you know the actual root cause.

I've had many students come to me frustrated because they just lost a match. They don't know why and don't yet know how to figure out the answer. I've found the best advice is to just ask questions. I lead them by asking *why* several times until we get to something we can work on.

Once you clear your head and are removed from the game enough to think objectively, the thought process could go a bit like this:

Why did you lose the game?

I lost because I didn't play my best…

Why didn't you play your best?

Because I missed too many easy bandejas and I played rubbish from the back.

Why did you play rubbish from the back and miss shots you usually hit with consistency?

I kept getting set up in the wrong place and I couldn't read the spin off the glass.

Why was the spin of the glass harder for you to read?

Well, I was playing against a lefty and I don't have enough experience here.

Solution: Play more games against left handers.

This is an extremely simplified example, but this exercise can lead to surprising insights if you follow the trail down deep enough. The point is to drill down to root causes and then create actionable next steps. Maybe you didn't get enough sleep, ran a 10K over the weekend, or played padel for ten days straight and just needed a break. Practise asking why on your own and with your partner to determine if you need to make a change to improve a certain area or if the loss can be chalked up to circumstances beyond your control.

The key here is to be willing to follow the *why* trail of questions all the way down to its conclusion and then work on that item, even if it might be difficult. If you really want to get better and play at a high level, be willing to embrace the challenge even if that means struggling through weaknesses.

How to Beat "Worse" Players

> *Use 'volume' as a tactic—play repetitively to the same player. [This is] not to put the other in the 'fridge', but to pressurise that player physically and mentally to force them to make mistakes.* —Andréas Johansson, Helsingborg.

To win matches against better players, you must first master the strategies for winning against weaker teams. One of the most surprising tidbits when it comes to elevating your game to the highest level is consistently beating teams who are worse than you. You must get used to being ahead, and knowing that any team can beat any other team on any given day. Even if you go up 5-0, 40-love, the game isn't over! You've got to maximise your ability to close out games and finish strong. Doing so will only help you later against better teams who will capitalise on slip ups.

Lose a point or two and the deadly thought of *I should be winning this game* creeps its way into your brain and you start to feel intense pressure to finish. If you don't experience this specific type of pressure on a regular basis you may not know what to do with it. Here are several practical steps I suggest for closing out games that you "should" win:

- **Don't rush:** When you lose a point and suddenly go to 5-1, don't just push on to the next point assuming you'll win. Take a few seconds and chat strategy with your partner. Take a deep breath, refocus, and clear your mind so you don't start making unforced errors. Work your strategy and don't rush the point. Wait for the right moment and then strike.

- **Be systematic:** Return to your roots of comfortable playing and systematically dispatching your opponents. You don't have to do anything crazy to win against weaker teams. Likely, if you keep the rally going and avoid unforced errors, you'll put yourself in a better position to win the point.

- **Don't cave to pressure:** Sometimes a weaker team will beat you. The games you "shouldn't have lost" end in defeat. Learn to ride these waves. You can only guarantee that you are trying your hardest in a game, and sometimes it won't be enough. Suffer defeat well and you will grow stronger as a padel player.

In one of the most well-respected and bestselling sports books of all time, *The Inner Game of Tennis*, W. Timothy Gallwey shares this about concerning yourself with the effort to win points:[9]

---

9 Gallwey, W. Timothy. The Inner Game of Tennis: The Ultimate Guide to the Mental Side of Peak Performance. New York, United States, Macmillan Publishers, 2014.

The difference between being concerned about winning and being concerned about making the effort to win may seem subtle, but in the effect there is a great difference. When I'm concerned only about winning, I'm caring about something that I can't wholly control. Whether I win or lose the external game is a result of my opponent's skill and effort as well as my own. When one is emotionally attached to results that he can't control, he tends to become anxious and then try too hard. But one can control the effort he puts into winning. One can always do the best he can at any given moment.

Sometimes, worse teams will beat you. Doing your best in any given moment is not something to baulk at. Winners certainly do their best when they come out on top, but losers are often trying just as hard. In a game where there will always be one winner and several losers, elevate yourself above the need for winning as the only positive outcome.

Beat Better Players

Champions aren't made in gyms. Champions are made from something they have deep inside of them; a desire, a dream, a vision. —Muhammad Ali

When you play against players who are better than you, the pressure disappears. If you lose, it's fine, you were expected to. If you win, great! The underdog reigns victorious. But remember, when you're playing against better players, the pressure is on them to perform at a high level. Use this to your advantage.

Here a few ways to elevate your game against better players:

- **Don't play their game:** Whether it's a tennis player with lightning-fast reflexes at the net, or a team with a strong defence against topspin smashes, don't submit to their game. Use a variety of strategies to win by varying your game and being unpredictable.

- **Slow the game down:** This strategy works on better players who might not have the patience padel requires. It will be less effective against experienced padel players, but there's never a disadvantage to slowing the game down to further analyse the other team. Use the lob often and make sure to mix it up with the chiquita as well. Master time and space on the court.

- **Be patient and play sensibly:** Beating players who are better than you is all about practising patience and being sensible. Great players have these traits in abundance. Be patient and play with angles. Be sensible by reading your opponents and using tactics that they find difficult to defend against.

As with any game in this exciting sport, adapt to the rhythm and needs of the match as it progresses. What worked to win the first set might not work in the next. As you adjust your strategy and your playstyle, the "enemy" is also making plans. They might come to the second set with an entirely different game plan. This is what makes sports exciting! Analyse and adjust on the fly for maximum success.

5 Steps to the Perfect Pre-Tournament Routine

Whether you're a seasoned padel expert who's played in countless competitions or you just booked your first competitive match, these secrets are for you. Between myself, our trainers, and the people we've coached in our growing community, we have a multitude of competition experience. One of the most common questions we get is, "How do I get ready for my match?" Here are five quick tips for organising yourself for competition. Some of these might appear obvious at first look, but professional players have mastered each step.

1. **Have your bag packed and ready to go**

Make sure everything you need to play at your best is readily available to you. All the following are important pieces of gear to remember to pack: A main racket and a backup ready for competition, a wristband, headband, hat, sunglasses, towel, two or three spare overgrips, balls, chalk or magnesium powder if needed to keep your hands dry, extra socks, clean shirt, etc.

The key is not the will to win. Everybody has that. It is the will to prepare to win that is important. —Bobby Knight

Check that everything is in order and ready to go. Test your shoes for any deformities prior to the day of the match. It does you no good to come to the tournament lacking an important item. If you do this step first, you'll know what you might be missing and can plan accordingly to get what you need throughout the week.

2. **Sleep well and get your diet right**

Do you think Bela downs a huge portion of fish and chips before he plays? Would you catch Galán snacking on Doritos between points? No, of course not. Do you think Marta Ortega stays up all night playing video games? Most likely not. Eat a balanced diet throughout the week and eat light before the match to ensure you're in the best possible state to win. Regularly get at least eight hours of sleep per night leading up to the match so you come with maximum stamina.

The higher your level, the more mental and physical fatigue you will face as the match progresses. Players at the top make sure their body is in top physical condition so they can strategize, read their opponents, and make adjustments as needed throughout the game.

3. **Train the right way during the week**

The most important focal points for your training during the week are working on technical shots and getting good match practice. Take lessons with your coach to work on technique and join high-level competitions at a local club or with friends.

Exercise outside of the padel court two to three times during the week but don't overdo it. Make sure your mind and body are ready to launch into competition mode once you step out on the court. Play these warm-up matches before the competition with an intensity that might scare your opponents.

4. **Don't get overexcited about your match**

Do you find it hard to think about anything else other than your upcoming match? You're in good company! This is common in padel. It's important not to get so into it that we place too much time and attention in one place. It's very easy to get so anxious and stressed about the game that when it finally comes around you're a nervous wreck and play terribly. Preparation is fantastic, but it's certainly possible to go overboard as well. You can't play well if you're overzealous. It takes a calm approach to access the consistency necessary to win points at a higher level of play.

It's okay to be excited and to look forward to your game, but try not to get too agitated or too into it. Yes, padel is fun, but the outcome is not everything. Stay loose and know that no matter what, padel is fun. Give it your all on the court, but don't stress to such a high degree that you don't enjoy the time.

5. **Plan your week**

Planning your week is by far the most obvious tactic, but also the most commonly underused. Schedule your weekly agenda around your match. Try not to stay out late with friends the night before and don't schedule a work meeting the morning of your match. Create a margin of time around the competition so you don't feel rushed or pressured. Plan to show up early and work out all the details beforehand so you can focus on doing what you do best.

Set up a time at the beginning of the week to check in with your personal goals and how they align with your upcoming schedule. Plan the events you know will help you make progress and prepare you for the competition ahead.

When competing in a padel competition, it's important to lose well. This means not letting your emotions get the best of you and always being respectful of your opponents. Elevate your partnership by working together as a team and supporting each other on the court. If things don't go your way, ask *why* repeatedly to improve your game. Beat worse players by playing smart and utilising your strengths. Win against better players by improving your ability to adapt to a game as it progresses. Lastly, prepare your week before the competition by getting plenty of rest, eating well, and meticulously planning a solid pre-match routine.

Get on the Court

Reflection: *How did I take my last loss? How could I get more from the matches I lose?*

Action: *Write these reflections down, like a match report, and share it in our community so we can celebrate/commiserate with you!*

CHAPTER TWELVE
High-Level Competition Skills and Tactics

Champions keep playing until they get it right.
—Billie Jean King, professional tennis player

P ractise high-level skills and implement timely tactics and you will soon become a master at this game. In order to be competitive and work your way up the ranking system, it's important to develop a working understanding of the most difficult techniques and skills. Sure, you could have a coach standing by to assist you between points, but it's better to strengthen your ability to read the game and adjust on the fly. The most successful padel players are the ones who adapt their strategy to the needs of the specific game situation in order to come out on top.

This chapter shows you how to maximise your game so you can start winning and never stop.

Setting Up the Point

Back in part one we talked about the objective in padel; namely, to win the net so you can win the point. It's time to put this tactic into overdrive, while remembering the simplicity of how to win the game: Be the last team to hit the ball over the net. Master the setup volley and no one will be able to beat you.

In the back, your goal is to defend well to eventually take the net. Stay on your toes and return to ready position as quickly as possible to not give an inch. Vary your placement of the ball with a chiquita, a lob, or a more powerful shot to the body. Stay unpredictable by never being obvious about what you are going to do next. Once you have the opening to approach, move fast to close and then defend the net.

In the front, hit multiple setup volleys to put your opponent under pressure enough to deliver an easy ball you can destroy with impunity. It's this building of momentum for each point that is at once exhilarating, exhausting, and incredibly difficult to get right. It was the part of the game I struggled with the longest before I finally overcame it. It takes a duality of patience to avoid rushing to finish the point and timing to pull the trigger at the exact right moment. Learning to hit a great setup volley is key to winning at high-level competitions because it builds the point which makes your job of deciding when to hit a winner much easier.

The right setup volley is equal parts:

Moving your opponent: It probably goes without saying, but don't just hit an easy ball in front of your opponents hoping they will serve you up a gift. Give them an easy ball and you'll likely find yourself headed to the back of the court to defend the lob after losing the net. Instead, move your opposition around the court to open up space and give yourself time to adjust.

Varying speed and depth: If you hit too hard and flat, the ball will bounce too high off the back and will be easier to return. It's true that the higher level you go, the better everyone becomes defensively, but you can still force an easy ball by making it difficult for your opponent to decide what to do. For example, hit three or four balls to the middle with low speed and a bit of slice, and then find the sweet spot of landing your volley just before the line, forcing them to make a decision whether to move fast and take it before, or to risk a low bounce off the back glass that might be impossible to defend. Force your opponent into a split second of indecision and they might make a mistake.

Preparing for the winner: Once you force an easy ball, move forward into the net with intention. You did all the hard work to get to this point, so don't shy away now. If you pick the right ball to attack, you should be able to finish the point using a variety of shots at the net. Remember, sometimes it pays to play another safe setup volley deep into the middle. If you do get an easy ball, your opponents might start to come forward to defend against a strong smash. In this case, a basic setup volley to the middle of the court will actually score you an easy point with no risk.

On court, force yourself to slow down. Hit more setup volleys than you're used to. Move your opponents around with unpredictable shot variety, and only finish when a ball is so juicy you can't resist the urge to crush it.

Put Your Opponent in the Fridge

Brrr, it's cold in here!

One fun tactic I like to use on the court is to put one member of the other team in the metaphorical "fridge" to keep them cold. Spanish players invented this saying and use the strategy quite often. You can implement it for a single point within the game, but if you want to do it properly, it's best to do it for a series of points or even multiple games. I've seen this strategy work wonders, especially against teams that aren't as strong mentally, have a level mismatch, or if one member is stronger at the net and the other stronger in the back. If they rely too heavily on one person to finish the point, and the other is playing more defensively, it's a good idea to play more balls onto one player.

To put this strategy into a game, agree on a player to target with your partner. If you haven't yet played against these opponents, it's wise to play a few points to test their capabilities. Then, when a clear target emerges, move forward with your plan to ice out the stronger player by hitting the majority of balls to the weaker one. There's no hard-and-fast percentage, but if you have the opportunity to switch to their side, do it. Let them get tired playing defence, and then just when the moment feels right, hit a faster ball to the body or to the feet of the player who's now ice cold. Hopefully, if you time it right, the ice-cold player won't be ready to defend and you'll win the point.

Employing a tactic like this one works wonders because it gives you a focus for the match. No matter the result of the match, you came with a focused plan of attack, and this will only help to improve your strategic game as you continue to play. I like this devious manoeuvre because it demonstrates the complexity of strategy within a surprisingly deep well of possibilities. You can take this so many different directions and, to win higher-level games, you will need to. You have more control of the game than you realise, even when your opponents are more skilled or just happen to be winning 5-0 within the first ten minutes. Take a step back, analyse what's going on, slow the game down, and implement a new strategy. Don't just sigh and go back to the court expecting things to be different. You have nothing to lose at this point, so try something new.

At a good level, be aware that if you use this tactic you can sometimes be playing the weaker player into the match and they get more consistent the more you do it. Change tactics if your previous plan stops working. Put a player from the other team in the fridge to test their mental capacity and force them to adjust to your game. Then, pick simple strategies and execute your plan on the fly.

Defending the Fridge

Employing tactics like putting your opponent in the fridge will build your resilience when the same tactics are employed by the enemy. If the tables turn and you are the one getting the majority of balls, hit a high lob and move to the net. This forces your opponent to think twice if they want to hit it to you at the net, or instead hit it to your partner and thereby pull them out of the fridge.

The combination of tactics and mental side—the similarities between chess and padel, that's what I love most. —Majid Bin Obood, Dubai

Defending against this strategy, and other advanced tactics, means recognizing what's happening, coming up with an executable counterattack, and then doing it on the court. In-the-moment match analysis will come naturally over time, and you and your partner will find you can quickly adjust to anything the other team throws against you.

Use the Fence to Attack

Using the fence is a great weapon at your disposal. One major difference between intermediate players and more advanced players is the use of angles and the fence. We talked about this in an earlier section, but using the fence introduces an element of randomness into the game. You know this, as good players utilise the fence to turn the tide of battle their way. Well, now it's your turn to be one of those devilish players if you aren't already.

Be tactical in your approach to this shot. Each time you hit the ball over the net you should have a purpose for it. There needs to be a reason for what you are doing, unless you're desperately on the defensive and are just happy to hit it over. Hitting the fence on a short bounce doesn't need to be the end goal. Sure, it will work out sometimes that a fence shot is a winner, but more often than not your opponent will get to it and will suddenly be joining you at the net. It's not always the best idea to go for a fence shot, and it shouldn't become a shot you go for on every point.

With those caveats out of the way, the shot is truly effective when used at the right time and in the right way. You can hit to the fence with a soft chiquita from the back if there is space, but most of the time it will come in the form of an attacking volley from the net or a controlled setup ball.

Attacking Volley to the Fence

This is a shot you take from close to the net and hit aggressively, with slice, to ricochet off the fence with the hope the ball will die immediately. To attack this ball effectively, keep the racket head above the height of the ball, contact slightly in front of you, and follow through in the direction of the shot. The closer to the net you are, the easier the angle will be to hit an attacking volley, but also the less time you will have to adjust your position in relation to the oncoming ball.

Aim this shot relatively close to the fence but don't push too close because it's not worth the risk of the ball going out. Aim for hitting it up in the court where it's not easy for them to come in and block the ball before it hits the fence. The ball should bounce below the first horizontal bar on the fence so that it stays below net height so they can't attack you right back.

You'll play this ball cross-court most of the time, so left-side players will use their backhand, and right-side players will take this shot with a forehand. If the ball comes down the line, above shoulder height, and with medium to slow speed, this is the perfect opportunity to practise hitting aggressively down to the fence. Sometimes, if the ball comes down the middle of the court, you might have the angle to play to the fence with the opposite volley (forehand for left-side players and backhand for right), but this is less common because the angle is not as significant.

Controlled Setup Ball to the Fence

The controlled volley to the fence is less risky than its more aggressive counterpart, and is a great shot to practise. Consider it another version of the setup volley we discussed previously with the goal to set up the point to hopefully get an easier winner on the next rally. It likely won't finish the point unless you get a really lucky bounce, but the goal is to catch your opponent off guard.

Aim with precision closer to the fence than you would do with the aggressive shot. Hit close to the fence because if it's too far away, your opponent will just come in and block the ball. Hit a slow and accurate ball with a nice and calm body movement to maintain control and reduce risk.

Regardless of whether you hit an aggressive volley to the fence or opt for the more controlled version, stay alert. Immediately after you hit the ball, ready yourself at the net to finish the next ball, or to defend if the ball pops up too high. You must be ready for whatever happens because the fence can be fickle!

Many players, even at a high level, don't use the fence as often as they should. Put it into play with your game and make life difficult for your opponents.

The Vibora: An Attacking Slice Smash

The vibora is a shot unique to padel that feels great once you master it, but the process of learning it is quite challenging. If you're from tennis or haven't yet mastered the bandeja, the vibora might prove to be one of the most difficult shots to add to your repertoire. The vibora is an attacking smash versus its slower brother, the bandeja. However, it's great for advancing to the next level because it can be extremely difficult to defend if hit well. The purpose of the shot is to hit a ball into the corner that bounces off both glasses that your opponents will have a difficult time defending.

When it comes to deciding when to use this shot, look for a lob down the middle of the court. Typically, the vibora is hit by the left-side player more often than the right-side player because of starting court position and where lobs tend to go. So, if you're a left-side player, practise and get really comfortable with the Vibora. Get into the bandeja position, but instead of keeping your racket up and to the side, position it behind your head to generate the racket head speed you will need.

Picture an analog clock to envision where to hit the ball. 3 o'clock is the sweet spot for the vibora so that you can generate the right-side spin on the ball. You don't want too much top spin (1 o'clock) because the ball will bounce too high, nor do you want too much slice (5 o'clock) because you might end up hitting the ball out of the court with fast racket-head speed. You can either use your chest to control the ball, or you can extend your arm to try and come around, however, the majority of the spin will come from the arm as it extends around the ball.

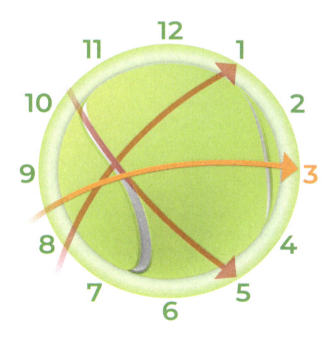

Image 13: The ball as a clock face.

The vibora is often a point finisher so practising in a match isn't always recommended, especially if you don't yet have confidence in your ability to hit it at 70%. It's best to practise with a basket of balls and a partner. Have them put ball after ball into the middle for you to practise getting the right combination of speed and spin. Eventually, if you are able, it's best to have your partner lob up a ball and then try to defend your vibora as if you were in a real game scenario. This will give you effective data so you can adjust your spin and speed appropriately to make it hard for them to return.

You'll know you hit this shot correctly when the ball starts to have a side spin and lots of effect as it comes off your racket and into the glass on the other side. Hit these spinning balls into the corner and you will make life very difficult for your opponents and, thus, win more games.

Drop Shots and Their Place in Padel

The drop volley is my favourite shot in padel, both when I am playing and when I am watching others. A well-executed drop volley invokes a feeling of immense satisfaction and unbridled joy. However, here are three caveats to consider before introducing it into your game because it's not recommended for every scenario:

1. First, at a beginner level, it's difficult to do this shot in a way that gives you an advantage in the game. In fact, at the recreational level it's a shot I see far too often. Players try to drop the volley short so that their opponent can't reach it, but 90% of the time it gives the other team easy access to the net putting the drop volleyer under immediate pressure.

2. Secondly, the drop shot is high risk, high reward. It's fun to try at recreational and intermediate levels, and can be extremely rewarding if it works, but it's often not necessary. And, more often than not, the attempt ends in an unforced error. You're likely much better served by hitting a setup volley to win the point than trying to hit the perfect drop shot that bounces back over the net to your own side.

3. Lastly, you can't continue to use it against good players and get away with it. The drop shot is what I call a surprise tactic, in that it's best used on unsuspecting opponents. It needs to be a shot you use when they least expect it while on their heels waiting for yet another setup volley to the middle of the court.

There are two ways to hit the drop volley. Either you can hit it with an exaggerated brush down the back of the ball so that it bounces back toward the net after going over, or by hitting a more controlled volley down to the fence as we discussed previously.

> *I have two favourite ways to win at padel: 1) A slow bajada to their feet or body forcing them to play a high floating ball. Then I volley it to the middle or to the empty space that ends in a double bounce and none of the players can touch it. 2) A slow to-the-feet chiquita that results in a high floating ball that I can place whenever I want and none of the players can touch it and it bounces twice. It's my favourite because it's a very "constructive" point. …It's important to know that you still have to play a volley or two to be able to win the point.* —Seif Abou Senna, Cairo

To hit the perfect drop volley, ensure you are in ready position at the net with your racket up. Keep your body compact with your elbow tucked into your body with your racket back. When you strike the ball, come under it with an extreme slice to create backspin by hitting the ball at the 6 o'clock position. Never let the ball bounce first with this shot because your opponents will have time to reposition themselves, and it becomes harder for you to disguise the shot as you are forced to come under the ball even farther.

Target as close to the net as possible, and as a guideline, aim for no more than a metre from the net. Any closer and the risk is far too great, and any farther back just gives your opponent an easier ball with which they will probably lob you. Time this shot perfectly and you're almost guaranteed a winner. Use it too often and you'll set yourself and your partner back in the match. Use the drop volley with extreme prejudice.

Develop a Consistent "Out by Three Metres" Kicksmash

With the right technique and practise, anyone can hit a ball off the back glass with spin so it bounces out the side of the court's three-metre fence. It's a myth that only taller tennis players are able to generate the power necessary to kick it out. In fact, it's not really about power at all, proper technique will generate the right amount of topspin. The kicksmash is a terrific shot to master because at most recreational clubs you aren't allowed to run out of the court to return the ball. So, if you are able to kick it out, you've automatically won the point.

The technique for this shot is similar to that of a tennis serve and the topspin smash to the fence you learned previously. This is the shot most familiar to tennis players and will likely feel much more natural than the bandeja or the vibora. From the ready position you move back into a "trophy position" to prepare your body to hit with full power by hitting through the legs and into your arm. Raise your non-racket hand to the sky, pointing to the ball, bend your legs, tilt your shoulders to get better range of motion, and get ready to release the coil of power you've channelled from your legs and core. Contact the ball above your head at the top part of the racket, different from most shots where you'd aim to contact in the middle of the racket face. As you hit the ball, follow through and brush away to generate even more spin so it will kick away from the glass to pop over the side fence.

Aim to hit the ball midway up the court so that it bounces high on the separation between the last two panels of back glass. The higher the bounce off the glass, the more the ball will kick off the back and fly out the side. And remember, you don't need an overwhelming amount of power with this shot. As many YouTubers have demonstrated, you can sit down in a chair in the middle of the court and still kick the ball out if you hit it with enough spin. Give this a go if you need to practise spin first so you can add power later. If you rely too heavily on power for this shot, it will be next to impossible to kicksmash if you happen to be using older balls, if the weather is cold and/or wet, or if you're playing on a slower court.

Practise hitting the ball slightly off the back glass with topspin. Get a feel for the technique in a controlled environment. Then, take a basket of balls to get the feeling of everything required to kick it out over the fence. If you struggle to find the right angle, exaggerate your approach by trying to hit the ball as far to your left side as possible. This will help generate the spin you need and will force your back to bend as well.

In a match, test it out on occasion, but only play to your comfort level. Don't try for a topspin smash from the back of court. Wait for just the right ball to come closer to the net. If you get an easy lob into the centre of the court, come under the ball with confidence, load up with your entire body, and hit it out. As soon as you hit it, return to ready position and get ready to defend the counterattack if one is forthcoming.

For competitions, especially when the other team is able to run out of the court to return the ball, use the kicksmash sparingly and intelligently. Even at near 100% accuracy, which is quite difficult to obtain, it's not always the best option. If your opponents are already running out of the court, hit a fake smash. Or make a move like you are going to hit the kicksmash, but switch to a controlled vibora at the last second. Hit it with full power and topspin so that it comes back over the net high and impossible to return. Change up your tactics to be unpredictable.

Popping the Ball Out with a Four Metre

This is the ultimate finisher in a padel game. It's called the *Four Metre* because the height of the back court glass and fence is four metres. Hit this shot from the net position with power and you will win the point every time. This is the shot you must be able to hit near 100% as you increase your level. If your opponents give you the easiest little floater the sport has ever seen, capitalise on the gift. Or, if you can get the timing just right, you can close the net early and hit the ball out on a softer and higher shot. When your opponents smash hard off the back glass and the ball is flying back over the net, finish with a four or three metre to turn the tables. You'll see this last type at the World Padel Tour level often because they read the ball so well and know exactly where to stand to counterattack.

The technique of this shot is to hit flat and down with no spin so that it bounces early on the other side of the court to have the right trajectory to bounce out. The farther you are from the net, the deeper the angle has to be to hit the ball out. So, if you have your opponent back on their heels and pressed from your attacks, edge closer to the net, and get ready to hit it out by four.

The key to getting this shot just right is near-perfect timing. Hitting it out by four requires early recognition and preparation. See the chance to hit it out and then get into the right position. When you get ready to hit the ball, make sure the racket is up to hit down on the ball, contact in front of you, and use a little bit of wrist to snap it out to the side or the very back of the court for the full four metres.

Smash Like Lebrón!

Sometimes students come to me and want me to teach them how to soar around the court like Coello, hit a lightning-fast vibora like Galán, or smash like Lebrón. Playing like the top-level players is not usually advisable because the risk of failure of consistency is so great. If you can't hit a perfect smash like Lebrón nine out of ten times, and instead hit it at only 50%, you're making way too many mistakes! If I played against you, I would take those odds and hit easy lobs to you every time. You'd not only lose more points than you'd win, you'd exhaust yourself doing so. It's more risky than it's worth to try to hit a smash from deep in the back of the court like Lebrón.

However, if you are ready to explore it and see if it's something you might want to add to your game, I'll show you how. If you can get to the point where the threat of your ability to smash from the back gives the other team pause, you've developed an additional bonus. This is the part of the reason why Lebrón performs so well and wins so many matches, not just because he hits this shot with consistency, but because he *can*. The fear of his incredible topspin smash changes the rest of the game in his favour.

Here are the five steps Lebrón does almost to perfection every time he hits the topspin smash from the back of the court:

1. **Lighting-fast into position**: With no delay whatsoever, he positions himself exactly where he needs to be.

2. **Spectacular knee bend**: He bends his knees extremely far so that he can drive up with incredible power through his legs.

3. **Shoulders pointing towards the back corner**: This gives him excellent rotation so that he can hit with power and spin.

4. **Back bent with extreme flexibility**: He is able to contact the ball far to his left side, which gives him the ability to contact the ball perfectly and naturally add spin.

5. **Contact point and brush are perfect**: He hits the ball in exactly the right part of the top end of the racket. The head speed and brush create the desired effect.

It will take lots of practice to put this smash into your game. Likely, it's not necessary at your level to work this in. It's not something I recommend unless you are already hitting the topspin smash regularly and easily within your game. But as you give it a go, adjust your technique, aim, and power level to the five steps above. Slowly work on it over time and, before you know it, you might have a new weapon.

Defending Out of the Court

Running outside of the court is one of the most exciting parts of padel. Especially when you consider the pro level and how often it happens during a game, it's every player's dream to get to this level of entertainment, both for themselves and for any onlookers. Most recreational clubs don't have the space required to let players run out of the court, but if you find yourself lucky enough to be playing on centre court and you're playing against a team with a powerful kicksmash, don't be caught off guard! You will quickly find this information not only relevant, but necessary.

If you've just hit a short lob and you can see your opponent with their legs bent and they're loading up for an aggressive topspin smash (and they've already proven they have the technique and power to be able to hit it out of the court) immediately sprint to the door. As you get to the door, be extra careful not to touch the net post or the net itself, because you will lose the point automatically. As you cross the threshold, turn to your left to face the ball to track it down and line up your next shot. Take aim straight back into the court, and even into the net if possible. If you don't have the right angle, pop the ball back over the fence to keep it in play. If their kicksmash doesn't go out and instead hits the fence, this is your partner's ball to cover for you. You can come back into the court to hit the ball, but they will likely be in a much better position to defend. As soon as possible, return to the court and get ready for wherever the ball might go next and do your best to keep the rally going.

To round out your mastery of the game of padel, always remember the necessity of building the point. Use advanced tactics like putting one member of the opposition in the fridge to take control of the game. Treat the fence like a powerful tool you can use to change up the game in your favour. Use drop shots with precision and deadly timing. Improve your smashes and develop a consistency with whatever shot you choose at any given time. Keep working on each area of your game, but always have patience with yourself as you grow.

• •

Get on the Court

Reflection: Do you go into each match with clear and simple strategies? (Most do not) Do you read and adjust to the game as it's going on?

Action: Why are you still reading a book? Get on the court, practise a new strategy, and start improving!

CONCLUSION
The Next Step of Your Journey

My journey in padel is transforming every day. It's different than it used to be but, surprisingly, even more enjoyable. Life is a series of comings and goings and we aren't meant to stay on one path forever. These days, I don't play as often as I used to. Instead, I spend my working hours creating in-depth padel content, coaching future WPT hopefuls, attending live events, and commentating on matches at every opportunity.

Wherever you find yourself in your own personal journey with this sport we are all obsessed with, I wish you perfect weather, sturdy equipment, and great friends to play with.

Coaching the GB National Junior team at the Junior World Championships.

Before you go, here are seven takeaways from this book. Pick just one or two and implement them into your game today. Mastery in the game of padel is a multistep process, but it need not take forever. Expedite your progress by keeping this book as a permanent fixture within your padel bag ready to reference at any moment. The following seven items are the gold standard all padel players must possess in order to improve and win:

1. **Increase self-awareness**: Know what you need to work on. Record your matches to give yourself an idea of vital next steps for improvement. Increasing your awareness of your current level will show your strengths and highlight your weaknesses. Work on advanced tactics and techniques, but don't skip the basics.

2. **Blend in-person coaching with online resources**: There is no replacement for an excellent coach who will help analyse your game and point you in the right direction. But ultimately, improvement is on you and how badly you want it. There are tons of great resources out there to learn and understand advanced parts of the game. For maximum output, find a great coach, but also make time for working on items on your own.

3. **Be intentional**: Have a plan for what you are going to focus on in your matches. Intentionality is the bread and butter for anyone looking to improve their level. Each time you step on the court, have a clear goal in mind for what you want to work on or think about during that game. This will not only help you improve that one thing, but it will help to focus your mind and keep your head in the game.

4. **Avoid injury**: Don't let your love of padel come to a crashing end because you injure yourself. Every time you step on the court, make sure you're warmed up and ready to go. If you feel fatigued, don't play. Take a few days off. If your arm is starting to hurt, especially in the elbow region, immediately stop. Don't push so hard for one night of fun and enjoyment and risk months of recovery where you're sitting on the couch texting *no* to every friend who asks if you're ready to play.

5. **Develop and master consistency**: If you can become a master of consistency, you will win most of your games. Patience infused with sensible play is how padel champions are made. Once you learn proper technique and have a solid grasp of the game, learn how to repeat each shot ten out of ten times, every time you step on the court.

6. **Integrate advanced tactics**: When you're playing in a high-level match, keep a careful eye on your opponents. Figure out their weaknesses, make a plan with your partner, and then capitalise on it to reign victorious. Remember to continue to adapt, because the enemy makes plans too!

7. **Get on the court**: No tip in this book will help to improve *your* padel game unless *you* take action and get on the court. Keep showing up with intention to improve, not just to win. Winning is secondary to improvement. You won't win every game, but you can take small steps toward growth at every opportunity.

I hope this book has been informative, entertaining, and helpful as you make progress in your own journey. I firmly believe that with dedication and practice, anyone can improve their skills and become a better player. Whether you hope to play competitively at a high level, pick up the mantle of coach, or your dream is to one day win the World Padel Tour, there is always room for improvement and growth.

Our journey together in this book has come to an end. Now the ultimate question is before you: Where are you going next?

To your growth and padel domination,

—Sandy

EVERYTHING YOU NEED TO TAKE THE NEXT STEP IN YOUR PADEL JOURNEY

Join ThePadelSchool.com for world-class training videos across all levels, access to a highly engaged community of fellow padel enthusiasts, and exclusive content only for members.

We can't wait to see you there as you continue your padel journey.

—Sandy and The Padel School team

A QUICK FAVOUR?

Before you go, can I ask you for a quick favour? Would you please leave this book a review wherever you purchased it?

It will only take a few minutes, and other padel enthusiasts just like you will find it easier to pick it up and read.

Thanks so much for your time!

ABOUT THE AUTHOR

Sandy Farquharson is the founder of The Padel School and has over a decade of professional padel coaching experience. Sandy and his team run coaching clinics around the world and coach players of every level - working with an average of over 3000 players per year. Sandy was responsible for designing and writing of the LTA's padel coach education program. To date, he has trained over 100 padel coaches across the world. Alongside his coaching experience Sandy plays for the GB Mens team (at the time of writing) and has represented GB for almost 10 years.

An entrepreneur at heart, Sandy is driven by his desire to grow the game of padel across the globe and to provide everyone with access to high-quality padel training advice.

Printed in Great Britain
by Amazon